Manna in the Morning

Nourishment from The Word of God

Jacqueline Renee Harts, M.A.

Nelson Publishers, Inc., Nashville, Tennessee, and The Message, Copyright © 1993, 1994, 1995, 1996, 2000, 2001, 2002. Used by permission of NavPress Publishing Group, Colorado Springs, CO 80935.

Copy Editor: Anita Palmer, The Strong Word Communication Services

www.xulonpress.com

To my husband who always supports me and encourages me to release my dreams.

To the Temecula Critique group of the San Diego Christian Writers Guild who helped me develop my writing skills.

To the members of my Bible Study group, family and friends who have enjoyed my e-mails.

Contents

II. Manna in the Morning: Nourishment from the New Testament

Day 364: Here I Am! • Day 365: In a War • Day 366: The New Jerusalem

Preface

Why Manna in the Morning?

God provided manna for the Israelites as they wandered in the desert for forty years. According to Exodus 16:4, it was bread from heaven. God's people were instructed to go out each day and gather enough for that day. It was their daily sustenance.

In much the same way, these devotions were composed each morning as I spent time with God in His Word. They provided nourishment for my spirit and gave me the strength I needed to get through the day. During these early morning times, God's Word clearly spoke to me and deeply ministered to my heart. God always knew precisely what I needed to hear and He spoke it to me so plainly through His Word. The messages blessed me so much I started writing them down and sending them out to members of my Bible study group as daily e-mails. The word I received from the Lord blessed them as well.

One evening, one of the ladies in the Bible study group bustled in and grumbled about how she had spent hours at the Christian bookstore unsuccessfully looking for a book like my e-mail messages. Her remark confirmed what I felt in my heart, that God wanted me to share these words with the world.

I have gathered the daily "manna" God gave me together and stuffed them into an imaginary bread basket—this book—to accompany you on this journey we call life. The Scriptures have been taken from every book in the Bible. It is my prayer that the words in this book would not just be words on a page, but that the Holy Scriptures would be a daily source of nourishment for you, as they were for me.

As you open this book to read a selection, think of yourself as famished. Picture yourself opening up a basket and breaking off a piece of bread, just enough to satisfy you for the day. Like the Israelites, you must gather the manna daily. In Matthew 6:11, Jesus instructs His disciples to ask God for their daily bread. As you feast on the manna, may it become alive and active in your heart as it did for me. May God open your ears to hear His voice gently speaking to you throughout the pages of this book. My desire and purpose in writing this book is for you to be drawn into a deeper, more intimate relationship with God and with His Word.

Jacqueline R. Harts
Perris, California
September 2007

About the Author

Jacqueline has a Master of Arts in Counseling Psychology from National University. Her compassion for people and her sensitivity to the emotional needs of others gave her the desire to help relieve their suffering hearts. It was this desire and a quest to gain a better understanding of herself that led her to study psychology. She uses her knowledge of psychology in her relationships with others, and it is the background that influences the way she thinks and writes.

Jacqueline found herself trying to answer the two questions that everyone eventually faces: "Who am I?" and "Why am I here?" As a result of two co-workers witnessing to her, Jacqueline opened the door of her heart and gave her life to Jesus Christ on December 5, 1989, at the age of twenty-five. It was in her relationship with Jesus that she found the answers to those two very important questions.

Jacqueline loves the Word of God and enjoys reading through the Bible each year. The Scriptures have been very instrumental in her life. During times of depression they lifted her spirit. When she had lost all hope and was being bombarded with suicidal thoughts she found hope in the Word of God. When she was wandering aimlessly through life the Scriptures gave her direction and purpose. She is amazed at how she finds new things in the Bible each year. God faithfully uses His Word to meet her right where she is. As an encourager in the body of Christ, Jacqueline uses God's Word to comfort others with the same comfort she receives from God through His Word.

Jacqueline is a wife, mother, and career woman. In addition, she and her husband, Arthur, are entrepreneurs and founders of Harts Enterprises, Inc. The Harts are longtime residents of Southern California and have been attending New Venture Christian Fellowship in Oceanside, California, for more than ten years. Jacqueline is a free-lance writer and an accredited member of the San Diego Christian Writers Guild.

Day 1: Are You Hiding?

Then the man and his wife heard the sound of the LORD God as he was walking in the garden in the cool of the day, and they hid from the LORD God among the trees of the garden.

—Genesis 3:8-9 (NIV)

Adam and Eve hid from the LORD because, as a result of their disobedience, they became painfully aware of their nakedness. Our sin may cause us to feel ashamed and to try to hide from God as well. However, we can never really hide from God. Nothing is hidden from the eyes of the LORD.

Do not think you can harbor something in your heart away from the knowledge of God. If you have hatred in your heart toward someone, the other person may not know it, but God is well aware. He knows the condition of your heart better than you do. As difficult as it may be when you miss the mark, be willing to go to the heavenly Father and admit the wrongdoing. Confess your sins and turn away from them. The sooner you get back into fellowship with the LORD, the better off you will be.

Sin may be pleasurable for a season but in the end it leads to death. Adam and Eve probably enjoyed the fruit of which they partook, but look at the price they actually paid. Not only did their sin get them cast out of the Garden of Eden, the true paradise, it also led to death.

Come out of hiding today. Remove the barriers between you and God and experience the grace and mercy He so generously gives. Let go of the shame and guilt and come out of the darkness. Dwell in the light with your heavenly Father.

Manna Moment

Are you attempting to hide something from the LORD? If so, be honest and open and confess the sin to Him. Enjoy the experience of being released from bondage, fear, shame and guilt. Freedom from sin is like having a gigantic boulder removed from your shoulders.

Day 2: Enjoy a Close Relationship

Enoch lived 365 years in all. He enjoyed a close relationship with God throughout his life. Then suddenly, he disappeared because God took him.
—Genesis 5:23-24 (NLT)

Enoch enjoyed a close relationship with God all of the 365 years he lived on earth. We cannot change what we did in the days that are behind us, but we can take the steps to enjoy a close relationship with God all the days we have yet to live. Devote time to draw closer to Him each and every day.

We want to be close to God so we can hear His voice when He whispers ever so gently. Jesus has called us friends (John 15:14-15). He is the faithful friend who sticks closer to us than a brother. We are capable of sharing an intimate relationship like Jesus and the Father, so close that the two become one, Jesus in you and you in Him. Be like Enoch and enjoy a close relationship with God for the rest of your life.

Manna Moment

Think about your closest, best friend on earth. Recall the good times you have shared. Think about the difficult times you supported each other through. Now carry that over into your relationship with Jesus. Confide in Him. Tell Him your deepest, darkest secrets. Cry out to Him in the difficult times and rejoice with the Lord in the good times.

Day 3: Is Anything Too Hard?

Then the LORD said to Abraham, "Why did Sarah laugh and say, 'Will I really have a child, now that I am old?' Is anything too hard for the LORD? I will return to you at the appointed time next year and Sarah will have a son."
—Genesis 18:13-14 (NIV)

Is anything too hard for the LORD? He is the One who gave Sarah a son when she was well past the age of childbearing. Sarah was 90 years old and Abraham was 100 years old (Genesis 17:17). Our God is still in the business of working miracles.

If God produced life from a barren womb, surely He can bring life to a dead or stale situation in your life. Whatever circumstance you face today, it is not too difficult for the LORD to take care of. He handles all things at their appointed time. He can take the emptiness within you and fill it with life, love and joy. Praise God that nothing is too hard for Him.

Manna Moment

Are you in need of a miracle? Ask Him. Nothing is too hard for the LORD!

Day 4: Don't Look Back

Then the LORD rained down burning sulfur on Sodom and Gomorrah - from the LORD out of the heavens.
But Lot's wife looked back, and she became a pillar of salt.
—Genesis 19:24, 26 (NIV)

Two angels warned Lot and his family before the cities of Sodom and Gomorrah were destroyed not to look back. However, Lot's wife failed to heed these words. She looked back and became a pillar of salt.

This incident with Lot's wife illustrates the futility of looking back. It is pointless to look back and long for things to be the way they were. It is just as ineffective to look back with regret and wish we had done things differently. We cannot change the past. It is forever etched onto the walls of history. As we begin each new day, may we be like the Apostle Paul, in Philippians 3:13, and forget what lies behind us and press on toward what lies ahead.

Let go of regrets, grudges and debts you feel are owed to you. Cut the strings that tie you to the past and start each new day with a fresh perspective. Live your life in the present, focused on what you can do today to improve the quality of your life and the lives of those around you.

Manna Moment

Take some time each morning to plan your day. Ask God to show you what priorities He has for you.

Day 5: It Will Be Provided

Abraham looked up and there in a thicket he saw a ram caught by its horns. He went over and took the ram and sacrificed it as a burnt offering instead of his son. So Abraham called that place The LORD Will Provide. And to this day it is said, "On the mountain of the LORD it will be provided."
—Genesis 22:13-14 (NIV)

Another name for God is Jehovah Jireh, which means God, the Provider. Whatever we need, God will provide. If we are sick, He provides healing. If we are anxious, He provides tranquil peace. Should we find ourselves in a state of confusion, He gives direction. If we are depressed or sad, He will be our joy. In times of hunger or thirst, He is the Bread of Life and the Living Water.

Not only is God faithful to provide our necessities, He also fulfills our desires or wants. The Apostle Paul tells us God richly provides us with everything for our enjoyment (1 Timothy 6:17). Dwell on the mountain of the LORD and it will be provided.

Manna Moment

Make a list of all you would like God to provide purely for your enjoyment. Make sure what you want lines up with His Word and His will. Let your needs and desires be known to God and wait for Him to provide.

Day 6: A Certain Place

Jacob left Beersheba and set out for Haran. When he reached a certain place, he stopped for the night because the sun had set. Taking one of the stones there, he put it under his head and lay down to sleep.

When Jacob awoke from his sleep, he thought, "Surely the LORD is in this place, and I was not aware of it."
—Genesis 28:10, 11, 16 (NIV)

When we reach "a certain place" in our lives, we may be like Jacob and stop for the night. We might be tired and weary. We may be alone. It may be a familiar place. It may be a lonely place. Perhaps it is a place of confusion. It may be a cold place with a harsh environment. It might be a place where we doubt that anyone understands or even cares. It could be a place of darkness, where depression lurks in the shadows. It may be a place of deep pain and sorrow. Have you been there?

Whatever place you are in, remember the LORD is in that place with you. He is Jehovah Shammah, the God who is there. He has not left you or forsaken you. May you always be mindful of the LORD's presence.

Manna Moment

What place are you in today? Are you aware of the LORD's presence in this place? Send up an offering of praise for His presence in your place.

Day 7: "I Cannot Do It, but God..."

Pharaoh said to Joseph, "I had a dream, and no one can interpret it. But I have heard it said of you that when you hear a dream you can interpret it." "I cannot do it," Joseph replied to Pharaoh, "but God will give Pharaoh the answer he desires."
—Genesis 41:15-16 (NIV)

There are times in our lives when we must admit, "I cannot do it." When the seemingly impossible situations come, we need to throw our hands up in the air, cry out to God, admit that we cannot do it, and ask for His help.

We must rely on the same faith Joseph relied on…the faith of Almighty God. God will do it. He will give the answer. God will provide strength and impart wisdom. He will give direction and open the door for you. He will remove fear and doubt. In Mark 9:23, Jesus says, "Everything is possible for him who believes." Believe. And may God help you overcome any unbelief.

Manna Moment

When you hit a wall, be honest and acknowledge that you cannot do it. Implore God to give you the answer.

Day 8: God Will Help You

The LORD said to him, "Who gave man his mouth? Who makes him deaf or mute? Who gives him sight or makes him blind? Is it not I, the LORD? Now go; I will help you speak and will teach you what to say."
—Exodus 4:11-12 (NIV)

When Moses was in the desert and came upon the burning bush, he was right where God wanted him. Today, you are right where God wants you. The LORD has allowed whatever situation you are in and whatever circumstances you are facing right now, for a reason.

He will tell you when to go and how to go. When the appointed time comes He will tell you where to go. You might be like Moses and doubt if you have the adequate skills to fulfill God's request. However, He will help you, just like He helped Moses face Pharaoh. The LORD will equip you with all you need to accomplish the task He has given you.

Manna Moment

Are you looking for a solution to some problem? Seek help from the LORD.

Day 9: He Fights for You

Moses answered the people, "Do not be afraid. Stand firm and you will see the deliverance the LORD will bring you today. The Egyptians you see today you will never see again. The LORD will fight for you; you need only to be still"

—Exodus 14:13-14 (NIV)

In the midst of the battles you face, do not let fear grip you. Do not be afraid when your enemy chases after you. The LORD delivered the Israelites from the Egyptians and He will deliver you from your adversaries.

Instead of running around in a panic, stand firm on the Rock, Jesus Christ, our Savior. Stand strong, fully trusting in the LORD who fights for you. Be still in His presence and wait. He will confront the enemy and fight the battle for you.

Manna Moment

When you find yourself wrestling with the enemy, stop and give the battle to the LORD. Make the following declaration: "I thank You LORD that You fight for me and I need only to be still. I will stand firm in faith until You give me the victory in this situation."

Day 10: From Bitter to Sweet

Then Moses led Israel from the Red Sea and they went into the Desert of Shur. For three days they traveled in the desert without finding water. When they came to Marah, they could not drink its water because it was bitter. (That is why the place is called Marah.) So the people grumbled against Moses, saying, "What are we to drink?" Then Moses cried out to the LORD, and the LORD showed him a piece of wood. He threw it into the water, and the water became sweet.
—Exodus 15:22-25 (NIV)

Sometimes on our journey through life we must go through the desert. We get weary in the dry, hot days of desert wandering. In the course of traveling through the desert we encounter bitter waters: some pain, some disappointment, and some heartbreak.

When we cry out to the LORD, He changes our bitter to sweet. He turns our sorrow into joy. He takes our broken heart and makes it whole again. And we know all things work together for good to those who love God (Romans 8:28 NKJV).

Manna Moment

When your life is like biting into a lemon (very bitter) bear in mind that after God is done, when he has added the water and the sugar, your life will be refreshing, like drinking a glass of cold lemonade.

Day 11: A Place Prepared

"See, I am sending an angel ahead of you to guard you along the way and to bring you to the place I have prepared."
—Exodus 23:20 (NIV)

Just as God took care of His people, the Israelites, He takes care of His people today. He sends angels ahead of us to guard us as we walk along the path He has laid out for each one of us. God has prepared a place for each one of His people.

It is a place of peace and abundant joy. It is a place where His love is deeper and wider than we ever imagined. It is a place where the glory of the Lord dwells. Hallelujah!

Manna Moment

Follow the LORD as He leads you from day to day to the place He has prepared for you.

Day 12: His Glory

Then the LORD said, "There is a place near me where you may stand on a rock. When my glory passes by, I will put you in a cleft in the rock and cover you with my hand until I have passed by. Then I will remove my hand and you will see my back; but my face must not be seen."
— Exodus 33:21-23 (NIV)

We do not have to be like Moses and hide in the cleft of a rock from the LORD. If you are hiding from the LORD today, come out! Come out into the light.

In Isaiah 2:5, the prophet Isaiah encourages us to walk in the light of the LORD. When we accepted God's only Son, Jesus Christ, He came to dwell in our hearts. His glory lives on the inside of us. The glory of God is beautiful and magnificent. His brilliant light shines through us. We are to be a light in the darkness of this world.

Manna Moment

Walk in the radiant light of the LORD and let His glory shine through you.

Day 13: Compassion, Grace and Love

*And he passed in front of Moses, proclaiming,
"The LORD, the LORD, the compassionate
and gracious God, slow to anger, abounding
in love and faithfulness, maintaining love to
thousands, and forgiving wickedness, rebellion and sin."*
—Exodus 34:6-7 (NIV)

Our God is compassionate. He is concerned with every minute detail of your life, down to the very hairs on your head.

In compassion, He lifts us up when we are down and restores us to health when we are ill. Our God is wonderfully gracious. He gives us unmerited favor. He is slow to get angry and always forgiving. He pours His love on us in abundance. He loves us so much, He sent His only Son to earth as a sacrifice, in order to give us eternal life so we could be with Him in Heaven forever. Praise the name of the LORD!

Manna Moment

How has the LORD touched you with His compassion, grace and love?

Day 14: First Place

*Do not worship any other god, for the LORD,
whose name is Jealous, is a jealous God.*
—Exodus 34:14 (NIV)

Our God is a jealous God. That means He must be first in our lives and in our hearts. He does not want second or third place. He does not want to come after your children, your spouse or your career.

Psalm 37:4 tells us to delight ourselves in the LORD and He will give us the desires of our hearts. God only wants the best for us. He is the best. He knows that anything else we choose to put first will only leave us empty, disappointed and unfulfilled. Ensure that God is first place in your life and enjoy the best.

Manna Moment

What are you tempted to put before God? Whatever it is, it will be more enhanced in God's hands.

Day 15: The Glory of the LORD

Moses and Aaron then went into the Tent of Meeting. When they came out, they blessed the people; and the glory of the LORD appeared to all the people. Fire came out from the presence of the LORD and consumed the burnt offering and the fat portions on the altar. And when all the people saw it, they shouted for joy and fell facedown.
                              —Leviticus 9:23-24 (NIV)

The LORD Almighty is the King of glory (Psalm 24:10). In the above account the glory of the LORD was revealed along with a consuming fire. God appeared to the Israelites after they had prepared an offering. In 2 Chronicles 5:13-14, when the glory of the LORD filled the temple of God it was accompanied with a visible cloud. This time God's glory descended while His people were singing praises to Him. As we worship Him from the depths of our heart, His glory fills the temple of our hearts.

Jesus said the time has now come when true worshipers will worship the Father in spirit and truth. We worship Father God in spirit when we live according to His Holy Spirit who dwells within us. Real worship takes place when we walk in the truth of His Word. We worship the LORD when we honor Him and give Him the respect, adoration and devotion due His name.

Manna Moment

Dedicate some time to worship the LORD. Worship Him in the manner His Spirit leads you to. Whether you stand, sit or lie down, sing, or remain silent is not significant. The key factor is putting your entire heart into it. Worship Him alone, with all of your heart and you will be filled with the glory of the LORD.

Day 16: He Brought You Up

I am the LORD who brought you up out of Egypt to be your God; therefore be holy, because I am holy.
—Leviticus 11:45 (NIV)

God delivered the Israelites from physical slavery. In contrast, God brought us out of the land of spiritual and emotional slavery where the devil held us captive.

We were without hope, full of fear and sorrow and living discouraged and defeated lives. We were dead in our transgressions and he saved us and made us alive with Christ. The LORD brought us out of the world and its ways to be our God. He calls us to be holy as He is holy. He raises us up with Christ and seats us in the heavenly realms in Christ Jesus (Ephesians 2:6). Allow Him be the LORD of your life.

Manna Moment

Regularly visualize yourself occupying the land of prosperity, abundance, and good health. Take possession of the good land the LORD has for you by speaking it out of your mouth as if it has already happened.

Day 17: He Walks Among Us

I will walk among you and be your God, and you will be my people.
—Leviticus 26:12 (NIV)

Our God is not far off. He walks among us. God is there to catch us when we fall and pick us up when we stumble. He walks in the midst of us, like He did with Adam and Eve in the Garden of Eden.

As we walk with God we build a personal relationship with Him and get to know Him more intimately. When He walks among us, God has a destination in mind and He leads us on the narrow road that leads to abundant life and eternal life. He is our God and we are His people. You are blessed because you are a child of God and He walks with you.

Manna Moment

Take a walk today and allow thoughts of God walking with you to occupy your mind.

Day 18: At His Command

Whenever the cloud lifted from above the Tent, the Israelites set out; wherever the cloud settled, the Israelites encamped. At the LORD's command the Israelites set out, and at his command they encamped. As long as the cloud stayed over the tabernacle, they remained in camp.
—Numbers 9:17-18 (NIV)

We do not have a visible cloud to watch, like the Israelites did, but we do have the Holy Spirit. When we are genuinely seeking the LORD's will in our lives we will feel the gentle tug of the Holy Spirit in our hearts, leading us in the way we are to go. At the LORD's command we are supposed to go and at His command we are to stay. When the LORD says speak, we ought to speak the words He puts in our mouths. When the LORD doesn't give us the words to speak, we probably need to be quiet and listen. When the LORD says to love our enemies, we are to embrace them with a loving and forgiving heart. When the LORD says to give, let us give freely and generously, with a joyful spirit.

What happens when we let go of our will and surrender to the LORD? We experience true blessings. Our joy overflows and we have a deep sense of peace. He blesses the work of our hands and gives us success. He gives us favor and causes us to be fruitful. Whatever you do today, may it be at His command and may His blessings fill your cup.

Manna Moment

What has the LORD commanded you to do? Have you complied with His request?

Day 19: Do It His Way

The LORD said to Moses, "Take the staff, and you and your brother Aaron gather the assembly together. Speak to that rock before their eyes and it will pour out its water. You will bring water out of the rock for the community so they and their livestock can drink."

Then Moses raised his arm and struck the rock twice with his staff. Water gushed out, and the community and their livestock drank.

—Numbers 20:7, 8, 11 (NIV)

When the LORD instructs us, we must follow His instructions carefully. Moses was told to *speak* to the rock, instead he *struck* the rock twice. Perhaps he was so frustrated with the complaining, quarreling and rebellious attitude of the Israelites he got caught up in emotion and lost self-control. Unfortunately, after forty years of wandering in the wilderness Moses did not get to step a foot on the Promised Land because of this disobedient act. He was only able to look at it from afar.

The lesson we can learn from the example of Moses is to carefully follow the direction the LORD gives us. As a result of obedience we enter the good land He has for us and we are able to enjoy the fruit of the land. He has plans for each one of us for good and not for harm.

This passage also shows us a wonderful aspect of God's grace and love. It shows us that even when we try to do things our way, God is still faithful and provides for our needs. Even though Moses hit the rock instead of speaking to it, God still provided the water the Israelites needed to survive in the desert. God is so good.

Manna Moment

When have you been tempted to do something your way instead of the LORD's way? Did it work as well as you planned? As we do things His way, we find His way is the best.

Day 20: He Will Meet You There

Then Balaam said to Balak, "Stand here by your burnt offerings, and I will go to see if the LORD will respond to me. Then I will tell you whatever he reveals to me." So Balaam went alone to the top of a hill, and God met him there.

—Numbers 23:3-4 (NLT)

I encourage you today, to go to your favorite place and invite God to meet you there. Spend time alone with your Heavenly Father just to enjoy His Presence and give Him praise. It may be your favorite room in the house or along the seashore. Maybe you prefer to go on top of a mountain or in the woods. God will meet you wherever you choose.

If you seek Him, you will find Him. He does not hide from us. He does not get to busy to fellowship with us. The LORD does not turn His back on us. We, as His beloved children are always at the top of His list.

Manna Moment

Do you have a special place where you meet with God on a regular basis? Choose a comfortable place where you will be free from distractions and interruptions.

Day 21: God Fulfills His Promises

*God is not a man, that he should lie, nor a son
of man, that he should change his mind. Does
he speak and then not act? Does he promise
and not fulfill?*
                                   —Numbers 23:19 (NIV)

Our God is a faithful God. What He speaks, He
brings to pass. His Word does not return to Him void.
He fulfills all His promises.

When He told Abraham all people on earth
would be blessed through him, He made it a reality
through Jesus Christ. He fulfilled every one of His
promises to the Israelites when He brought them into
the Promised Land of Canaan and gave them victory
over their enemies. Heaven and earth may pass away,
but the Word of God stands forever. Stand on His
Word and you will be standing on solid ground.

Manna Moment

Are you waiting for God to carry out a promise
He made to you? In the interim, read Psalm 37:4 out
loud at least three times a day until your dreams are
realized. It says, "Delight yourself in the LORD and
He will give you the desires of your heart."

Day 22: Follow Wholeheartedly

*'Because they have not followed me whole-
heartedly, not one of the men twenty years*

*old or more who came up out of Egypt will
see the land I promised on oath to Abraham,
Isaac and Jacob – not one except Caleb
son of Jephunneh the Kenizzite and Joshua
son of Nun, for they followed the LORD
wholeheartedly.'*

—Numbers 32:11-12 (NIV)

Following God wholeheartedly is key and essential if we are to thrive in our relationship with Him. He wants our whole heart. To help you follow the LORD wholeheartedly, picture yourself, drawing an imaginary line around your heart with the LORD in the center, seated on His throne, in all of His glory and majesty. As we live our lives and grow in Him, He occupies more of the circle that encloses our heart. Everyone else and everything else in our lives, that are important, are in the circle too, but we relate to them through Him.

For example, my spouse and my children are in my heart also, but I relate to them through my relationship with the LORD. I treat them with love, the way the LORD tells me to. When I go to work, I am working for the LORD. My choice of recreational activities is going to honor God. When I look at my circumstances, I look at them with faith, through God's eyes. I see abundance, good health, and eternal life.

If we filter everything through our relationship with the LORD, we will stay aligned with God's will and therefore, follow Him wholeheartedly.

Manna Moment

List all the people and things dear to your heart, including hobbies, collections, and so on. If you could only choose one, which one would you keep? Continue down the list until you have all of them in order of importance. Do your priorities reflect the amount of time and attention you give each one?

Day 23: Long Enough

The LORD our God said to us at Horeb, "You have stayed long enough at this mountain."
—Deuteronomy 1:6 (NIV)

After forty years of wandering in the desert, God told the Israelites it was time to break camp and advance into the hill country, to the mountains and along the coast.

Have you been wandering in desert terrain for years? What mountain lies before you? Is it a mountain of fear, worry and doubt? Is it a mountain of sickness and disease? Maybe it is a mountain of pride and rebellion. It does not matter what kind of mountain lies before you, God is saying you have been there long enough. He wants you to go in and take possession of the land He has called you to. He will be with you and He will help you just like He was with the Israelites and helped them settle in their promised land.

Let us inhabit the exceedingly good land the LORD has promised to each one of us. Dwell in the land where peace, joy and humility flow abundantly. Live in the land of good health and prosperity.

Manna Moment

What is your next step in advancing toward your promised land? Carry out that step and then proceed to the next one. Occupy your territory inch by inch.

Day 24: He Goes Before You

"But I said to you, 'Don't be afraid! The LORD your God is going before you. He will fight for you, just as you saw him do in Egypt. And you saw how the LORD your God cared for you again and again here in the wilderness, just as a father cares for his child. Now he has brought you to this place.'"
— Deuteronomy 1:29-31 (NLT)

The LORD always takes care of His people. He will take care of you in every situation and circumstance, just like He did with the Israelites. He has brought you to the place where you are today. Take comfort in knowing that whatever battles you face today, the LORD goes before you and He fights for you. You are a child of God, made with His very own hands and He cares for you just like a good father cares for His child.

Manna Moment

How has the LORD cared for you in different situations? Tell someone how God has shown His faithfulness to you.

Day 25: He Watches Over You

The LORD your God has blessed you in all the work of your hands. He has watched over your journey through this vast desert. These forty years the LORD your God has been with you, and you have not lacked anything.
— Deuteronomy 2:7 (NIV)

We can learn a lot about the LORD as we look at how He dealt with the Israelites. During their forty year journey in the desert, which began due to their lack of faith, the Lord watched over them and provided for all their needs. He provided water out of a rock. He gave them manna every morning for food. Neither their clothes nor their shoes wore out.

Our God does not change. He still watches over His people today and He still provides all our needs. As we journey through this life, sometimes we find ourselves in the desert, spiritually or emotionally dry. Sometimes we are soaring high on the mountaintop. Wherever you are today, the LORD is watching over you and charting your journey. You are not alone. He is providing for all your needs and you shall not lack anything.

Manna Moment

God has His eyes on you, not to condemn you when you do wrong, but to take care of you and keep you from harm. Retain this thought in the forefront of your mind.

Day 26: The LORD Is God

Acknowledge and take to heart this day that the LORD is God in heaven above and on the earth below. There is no other.
— Deuteronomy 4:39 (NIV)

The LORD is God in our lives. He is God at our work place. He is God in our homes. The LORD is God in our marriages and over our children. He is God and there is not another. Carry this knowledge from your head to your heart. He has the whole world in His hands. Praise the LORD!

Manna Moment

When you think you know a better, shorter or quicker way than the LORD's way, remember the LORD is God in heaven and on earth. He knows the past, present and future, therefore, He has the advantage of seeing the big picture. Trust in the LORD.

Day 27: Give Generously

If there is a poor man among your brothers...do not be hardhearted or tight-fisted toward your poor brother.
Give generously to him and do so without a grudging heart; then because of this the LORD your God will bless you in all your work and in everything you put your hand to. There will always be poor people in the land. Therefore I command you to be openhanded toward your brothers and toward the poor and needy in your land.
—Deuteronomy 15:7, 10-11 (NIV)

Jesus is the most excellent example of a giver. He gave His very life for us.

Freely we have received and freely we should give to our Christian brothers and sisters and also to unbelievers. God created and cares about every person on this earth. God created the rich man as well as the poor man. Always be openhanded and openhearted toward the poor and needy in your land. Giving generously will not only bless the one you give to but God will also bless you in all your work and in everything you put your hand to. Amen.

Manna Moment

When you see someone in need give generously to that person.

Day 28: Prosperous and Successful

"Do not let this Book of the Law depart from your mouth; meditate on it day and night, so that you may be careful to do everything written in it. Then you will be prosperous and successful."

—Joshua 1:8 (NIV)

Here is God's secret key to success and prosperity: His Word. If you want a prosperous and successful life, do what His Word tells you.

You may wonder how you can live a life of such obedience. By meditating on the Word day and night so you can speak the Word over every situation in your life. Spending time in the Word consistently helps us to know the Word and get it down into our heart. It also enables us to follow what is written in the Word.

Manna Moment

Write key scriptures that inspire and encourage you on little index cards. Review them when you are sitting in traffic or standing in lines.

Day 29: Be Strong and Courageous

"Have I not commanded you? Be strong and courageous. Do not be terrified; do not be discouraged, for the LORD your God will be with you wherever you go."

—Joshua 1:9 (NIV)

Be strong and courageous for the LORD, our God is with you wherever you go. You do not stand by yourself. Whatever challenges you face today, you do not have to face them alone. He is with you. Do not tremble in fear or get distressed. The LORD our God is your Helper. He gives you strength and courage.

Just as He helped Joshua and the Israelites conquer the land He promised to them, God will help you possess what He has called you to. If it is peace in your home you are fighting for, God is with you. If it is a relationship that needs to be reconciled, God is with you. Be strong and courageous because the Maker of heaven and earth stands with you!

Manna Moment

Are you facing a situation that is causing you to be terrified or discouraged? Meditate on the above Scripture which says, "God is with you wherever you go," until your heart is full of strength and courage.

Day 30: Every Promise Fulfilled

So the LORD gave Israel all the land he had sworn to give their forefathers, and they took possession of it and settled there. The LORD gave them rest on every side, just as he had sworn to their forefathers. Not one of their enemies withstood them; the LORD handed all their enemies over to them. Not one of all

> *the LORD's good promises to the house of
> Israel failed; every one was fulfilled.*
> —Joshua 21: 43-45 (NIV)

This passage of scripture exhibits the faithfulness of God. His faithfulness is complete. God did not fail to keep any of His promises to the Israelites. Likewise, He will fulfill every one of His promises to us. Let's take a look at some of the promises God has made to us.

Those who love God's law will have great peace and nothing will make them stumble (Psalm 119:165).

He will give grace to the humble (James 4:6).

If we give it will be given to us pressed down, shaken together and running over (Luke 6:38).

If we make the Most High our dwelling and the LORD our refuge then no harm will befall us and no disaster will come near our tent (Psalm 91:9-10).

If we cast our cares on the LORD, He will sustain us (Psalm 55:22).

He promises us that He will never leave us or forsake us (Hebrews 13:5).

Those who sow in tears will reap with songs of joy (Psalm 126:5).

All the promises God has made are "Yes" in Christ (2 Corinthians 1:20).

Manna Moment

Search God's Word until you find a promise that soothes your soul, comforts your heart and is music to your ears.

Day 31: Hold Fast to Him

"But be very careful to keep the command-ment and the law that Moses the servant of the LORD gave you: to love the LORD your God, to walk in all his ways, to obey his commands, to hold fast to him and to serve him with all your heart and all your soul."
                                        —Joshua 22:5 (NIV)

Joshua spoke these words to the Reubenites, the Gadites and the half-tribe of Manasseh before they left the land of Canaan to return to their own land in Gilead. He wanted the Israelites to remember the LORD. Years later, Jesus taught that the most impor-tant command was to love the LORD with all your heart, mind, soul and strength.

Even today, it is equally as important for us to remember to love the LORD our God with all of our heart and soul, and to walk in all his ways. If it is not His way, we do not want to tread there. We must be very certain to hold fast onto Him.

Get a good grip on the LORD with your hands, by lifting them towards heaven with a humble heart and acknowledging Him as the Lord of your life. Hold onto Him by praising Him with your mouth, talking to Him in prayer and giving thanks to Him for all He is doing in your life. Cling to the LORD with your mind, by reading the Word and letting it renew your mind. Hold firmly onto God with your heart by loving Him more than you love anything or anyone else and putting Him first in all you do. Praise the LORD!

Manna Moment

Picture yourself hanging from a branch over a huge, rocky cliff. As tightly as you would hold on to that branch for dear life is how tightly you need to hold fast onto the LORD.

Day 32: Choose Today

"So honor the LORD and serve him whole-heartedly. Put away forever the idols your ancestors worshiped when they lived beyond the Euphrates River and in Egypt. Serve the LORD alone. But if you are unwilling to serve the LORD, then choose today whom you will serve. Would you prefer the gods your ances-tors served beyond the Euphrates? Or will it be the gods of the Amorites in whose land you now live? But as for me and my family, we will serve the LORD."
                              —Joshua 24:14-15 (NLT)

Choose today whom you will serve. Each day we wake up we have a choice to make. We can choose to serve the living God, who made heaven and earth or we can serve our own fleshly desires. Serving our own fleshly desires may provide temporary gratification but no lasting satisfaction. It often leaves a void in us, a feeling of immense emptiness. Then in a desperate attempt to fill that God shaped hole inside of us, we plunge further into some activity for another quick fix. On this trek, the flesh will never get enough of what it craves…power, wealth, notoriety, security, and so on. It is a vicious cycle.

Serving the LORD must be done from the heart. When we serve the LORD, He alone sits on the throne of our hearts. Nothing is more important to us. Seeking God and doing His will come first on our list of priorities. We trust Him alone to fulfill all our needs, wants and desires. We acknowledge that He is Almighty God, the Creator of all things. We praise Him for all that He has done, is doing and all He will do in the future.

Manna Moment

When you wake up make a declaration saying, "Today, I choose to follow the LORD. As for me and my family, we will serve the LORD."

Day 33: Rise in Strength

"So may all your enemies perish, O LORD!
But may they who love you be like the sun
when it rises in its strength."
                                    — Judges 5:31 (NIV)

May you rise like the sun in its strength and declare the glory of the LORD. The LORD gives you strength to rise each day, just like He gives the sun its strength. The sun has its course the LORD sets for it and we have the course the LORD has given each one of us.

Whether you walk or run, stay on the course He has given you. The sun is not detoured from its path. Do not allow distractions to lead you away from the direction the LORD has given you. Rise in His strength and let the glory of the LORD shine through you, like it does the sun.

Manna Moment

The next time you see the sun shining pause and understand that the same strength that causes the sun to rise is available to you through the Holy Spirit who dwells inside of you.

Day 34: Go with the Strength You Have

Then the LORD turned to him and said, "Go with the strength you have and rescue Israel from the Midianites. I am sending you!"
—Judges 6:14 (NLT)

In the above passage of Scripture, the LORD is calling Gideon to rescue the Israelites from the Midianites, who had been oppressing them for seven years. The Midianites were so cruel the Israelites fled to the mountains, where they made hiding places for themselves in the caves and dens (Judges 6:2). When the LORD told Gideon he was to go and rescue His people, Gideon looked at all of his shortcomings. After that he proceeded to ask God for a sign two more times in Judges 6:36-37 and 39.

Occasionally we may be like Gideon. When the LORD puts it on our heart to do something, we start looking at all the reasons why we are not equipped. We go down the mental list of all our inadequacies and convince ourselves and attempt to convince the LORD that someone else is more equipped to complete the task.

If He tells us to give something away do we mimic Gideon's approach and start asking God to give us a sign if it is really His will? During these times we have to go with the strength we have. When the Lord sends us on a mission, we have to take that step of faith and go for it. He knows what we need to accomplish what He has called us to do and as always, He will provide. When He sends you, go with the strength you have.

Manna Moment

Think of a time when you thought you could go no further. Remember how God gave you the strength to continue on each step of the way?

Day 35: The LORD Is Peace

But the LORD said to him, "Peace! Do not be afraid. You are not going to die." So Gideon

built an altar to the LORD there and called it
The LORD is Peace.
—Judges 6:23-24 (NIV)

The LORD is peace. If you are experiencing any fear or anxiety you are too far away from the presence of the LORD. If you feel like you want to make war with someone who did you wrong, stop and draw near to the LORD.

When you draw close to Him, you become enveloped in His peace. In His presence you are comforted in the secure blanket of His peace. Just curl up inside and let your heart, mind and soul be anchored in His peace today. Let Him be your Jehovah Shalom, the LORD, my peace.

Manna Moment

Are you at peace internally as well as with others? As long as it depends on you, pursue peace with all people, including yourself.

Day 36: Seeking Direction

Then all the Israelites went up to Bethel and wept in the presence of the LORD and fasted until evening. They also brought burnt offerings and peace offerings to the LORD. And the Israelites went up seeking direction from the LORD. (In those days the Ark of the Covenant of God was in Bethel, and Phinehas son of Eleazar and grandson of Aaron was the priest.) The Israelites asked the LORD, "Should we fight against our relatives from Benjamin again or should we stop?" The LORD said, "Go! Tomorrow I will give you victory over them."

—Judges 20:26-28 (NLT)

We can never go wrong when we seek direction from the LORD before taking any action.

The offering He would have us bring to Him is our heart, open and eager to do His will. When we let go of our will, and earnestly seek His direction, we hear the still small voice of God in us, gently saying to us "This is the way, do this." When we follow His instructions God will give us the victory, just like He did with the Israelites.

Manna Moment

As you make your plans, set your goals, plot your strategies and develop creative ideas seek direction from the LORD before taking action.

Day 37: All Is Not Lost

"It is more bitter for me than for you, because the LORD's hand has gone out against me!"
—Ruth 1:13 (NIV)

Naomi felt very bitter after her husband and two sons died. When she returned to her homeland in Judah and the women exclaimed, "Can this be Naomi?" Her response was "Don't call me Naomi," she told them. "Call me Mara, because the Almighty has made my life very bitter. I went away full, but the LORD has brought me back empty" (Ruth 1:20-21). Naomi was so bitter about her misfortunes she could not see the good things in her life. Nor was she looking at her circumstances with eyes of faith.

If you are in a place where your life is very bitter and it feels like the hand of God has gone out against you, I encourage you to have faith. Keep believing in our Lord and Savior. If you have loved ones who have passed away and the LORD left you here, that means He has more work for you to do. If God has left you alive on this planet He is not done with you yet. He has a purpose for you to fulfill in your life.

Naomi had Ruth, a faithful daughter-in-law who loved her, clung to her and provided for her. However, God used Naomi to change the course of Ruth's life and put her in the bloodline of Jesus Christ (Matthew 1:3-6). Later on, Naomi experienced the pleasure of laying her grandson on her lap and caring for him.

When you are in the thin of thick things and your life is very bitter, remember that the LORD has plans for you to give you a future and a hope. When He empties your life, He will fill it again. All is not lost.

Manna Moment

If you are feeling hopeless about a certain situation in your life, list all the future possibilities of good things that could come out of the current circumstances.

Day 38: Our Redeemer

Boaz went over and said to Ruth, "Listen my daughter. Stay right here with us when you gather grain; don't go to any other fields. Stay right behind the women working in my field. See which part of the field they are harvesting, and then follow them. I have warned the young men not to bother you. And when you are thirsty, help yourself to the water they have drawn from the well."
—Ruth 2:8-9 (NLT)

This scripture paints a beautiful picture of Jesus. The words that Boaz, her kinsman redeemer, spoke to Ruth remind me of how Jesus Christ, our Redeemer, speaks to us. Jesus whispers to us, "Listen, my child, stay right here with us, the Father, Son and Holy Spirit." Boaz wanted Ruth to stay in his field and Jesus wants us to stay in His field. We are His sheep and He is our Shepherd. As the good shepherd, Jesus desires to keep careful watch over us. He does not want us wandering off of the path He has prepared for us. While Boaz warned the young men not to bother Ruth, Jesus warns the enemy of our soul that we belong to Him. He is our refuge. Boaz told Ruth to help herself to the water when she was thirsty. Jesus provides us with living water and He says to us "Drink."

The way that Boaz took care of Ruth and showed her remarkable kindness is similar to how Jesus compassionately takes care of us. Ruth was a widow with no one to take care of her. Boaz took care of Ruth and provided for her. Even though we may feel all alone, Jesus is our constant companion, who faithfully provides for our every need. Boaz redeemed Ruth and Jesus Christ redeemed us and gave us abundant life on earth and eternal life in heaven. Praise the LORD!

Manna Moment

As you go through your day, thank the Lord for each aspect of the abundant life He has given you.

Day 39: Keep On Praying

In bitterness of soul Hannah wept much and prayed to the LORD.
—1 Samuel 1:10 (NIV)

Hannah replied, "I am a woman who is deeply troubled. I have not been drinking wine or beer; I was pouring out my soul to the LORD. Do not take your servant for a wicked woman; I have been praying here out of my great anguish and grief."
—1 Samuel 1:15, 16 (NIV)

When we are deeply troubled, may we be like Hannah and pour out our souls to the LORD. In times of deep anguish and grief, keep on praying to the LORD. When our souls are bitter, may we turn to the LORD, instead of running from Him.

In 1 Samuel 1:19 the Word says the LORD remembered Hannah. He granted her what she asked of Him. He will remember you too. You have not been forgotten. Keep on praying.

Manna Moment

Let the world around you fade into the background. What situation tugs on your heartstrings? Pray, focused on what is troubling you. It may be a prayer for personal needs or for the needs of someone else.

Day 40: Our Rock

"There is no one holy like the LORD; there is no one besides you; there is no Rock like our God."
— 1 Samuel 2:2 (NIV)

There is no one besides the LORD our God. If we do not have an intimate relationship with Him everything else in our lives is on shifting sand, with no eternal value.

Our God is a Rock. We can stand on Him. He is strong and unbreakable. If we build the foundation of our lives on the Rock, then we will be able to withstand the storms of life. Our Rock is a lasting rock and He will stand throughout eternity. He is always there when we need Him. Hallelujah!

Manna Moment

Reflect on the greatness of our God. Consider the immense power He demonstrates in His creation of the earth and all that is in it. Think about the uniqueness and diversity of every person He has ever created. Praise Him.

Day 41: Your Servant Is Listening

The LORD came and stood there, calling as at the other times, "Samuel! Samuel!" Then Samuel said, "Speak, for your servant is listening."

—1 Samuel 3:10 (NIV)

How do you respond when you hear the LORD calling your name? What an appropriate response Samuel had to the LORD. When the LORD calls our name it is appropriate for us to listen if He is indeed the LORD of our lives. If we acknowledge Him as our LORD, there is nothing He can ask us that we will not be willing to do.

If you are taking the time to listen that implies your heart is willing to obey no matter what He says. Listen to the LORD with an open heart. Let His words fall on the good soil of your heart. Listen for His still small voice with a purpose to take action.

To be honest, there are things the LORD could ask me to do that would be difficult for me to say "Yes, LORD" to. For example, if He wanted me to bear another child now that I am in my forties, it would take a lot of prayer for my heart to say, "Yes, LORD." But that lets me know I have more work to do when it comes to truly letting God be the LORD of my life.

Manna Moment

Think of something the LORD has asked you to do that was difficult. Did you follow through in obedience? Did you complete the task? Why or Why not? If so, did you feel exhilarated and blessed by your obedience? If not, did you confess it as sin to the LORD and ask for forgiveness?

Day 42: Revelation Through the Word

The LORD continued to appear at Shiloh, and there he revealed himself to Samuel through his word.
                                        —1 Samuel 3:21 (NIV)

God reveals Himself through His Word. In Samuel's day it was primarily His spoken word and today we learn more about the LORD through His written Word. We learn about God's nature, His compassion, His faithfulness, His grace and His mercy. In the Holy Bible, God reveals how He cares for His people. If you build your life on the foundation of His Word all will go well with your soul.

Isaiah 40:8 tells us the Word of God stands forever. When we delve into the Holy Scriptures we learn a great deal about our Heavenly Father and His remarkable qualities. We relate more intimately to Him than to our earthly fathers and mothers. God knows us better than we know ourselves and He desires for us to know Him. Take time to examine the Word of God and you will see Him and His character more clearly.

Manna Moment

Which Scripture reveals an aspect of God that you appreciate the most? Read it.

Day 43: He Looks Upon His People

"About this time tomorrow I will send you a man from the land of Benjamin. Anoint him leader over my people Israel; he will deliver my people from the hand of the Philistines. I have looked upon my people, for their cry has reached me."
— 1 Samuel 9:16 (NIV)

Something wonderful happens when our cries reach the throne room of God. He sends deliverance. He makes a way of escape.

In the above passage, He sent Saul to deliver the Israelites from the hands of the Philistines. And

He still delivers His people from their enemies, today. God does not change. He is the same today, tomorrow and forever. He will always look upon His people when they cry out to Him. If you are crying out to Him today, He hears you and He will deliver you from all your distresses.

Manna Moment

What is the cry of your heart? Lift it up to the LORD and expect Him to deliver you from all your troubles.

Day 44: Consider the Great Things

But be sure to fear the LORD and serve him faithfully with all your heart; consider what great things he has done for you.
— 1 Samuel 12:24 (NIV)

Stand in awe of the LORD and give Him the respect and admiration He is so worthy of. Serve Him faithfully as you fulfill the mission and dream He placed on the inside of you. Always consider what great things the LORD has done for you.

You slept last night with a roof over your head. He woke you up this morning. He gave you eyesight and the knowledge to be able to read this book. You are able to hear, feel, talk and taste. He has given you His love, grace and mercy. He fills our hearts with His joy and His peace.

Manna Moment

Take a moment to consider the great things the LORD has done for you.

Day 45: The LORD Looks at the Heart

But the LORD said to Samuel, "Do not consider his appearance or his height, for I have rejected him. The LORD does not look at the things man looks at. Man looks at the outward appearance, but the LORD looks at the heart."

—1 Samuel 16:7 (NIV)

We may be able to fool people with our outer appearances but we can never fool God. He looks at the heart. It is possible for us to do the right things with the wrong motivation. We may do the right thing only to receive praise from man or to compete with another person. To ensure that your motivations are pure set your heart on pleasing the LORD.

When the LORD looks at your heart may He see a reflection of the genuine love and true humility of Jesus Christ. As long as our hearts are humble and full of His compassion our actions will be motivated by love.

Manna Moment

What does the LORD see when He looks into your heart? Examine your heart and purge it of anything that does not flow with the loving nature of God.

Day 46: Stay Strong

Jonathan went to find David and encouraged him to stay strong in his faith in God. "Don't be afraid," Jonathan reassured him. "My father will never find you! You are going to be the king of Israel, and I will be next to you, as my father is well aware."
> —1 Samuel 23:16-17 (NLT)

When David was hiding in the wilderness his best friend Jonathan found him and encouraged him. Similarly, I encourage you, my friend, to be strong in your faith in God. Do not be afraid because the battle belongs to the LORD.

The LORD has plans for you, just like He did for David. They are plans for good and not for disaster, to give you a future and a hope (Jeremiah 29:11).

Manna Moment

When do you gain the most strength? Is it after a time of prayer, when singing a song of praise to the LORD, or while meditating on the Word? In order to stay strong, be sure to consistently spend time doing the activity which strengthens you the most.

Day 47: Find Strength

When David and his men came to Ziklag, they found it destroyed by fire and their wives and sons and daughters taken captive. So David and his men wept aloud until they had no strength left to weep.

David was greatly distressed because the men were talking of stoning him; each one was bitter in spirit because of his sons and daughters. But David found strength in the LORD his God.

—1 Samuel 30:3, 4, 6 (NIV)

When you feel like your world is destroyed...

When it feels like those you love have suddenly been snatched out of your life...

When you are greatly distressed and bitter in spirit...

When you have wept until you can weep no more...

Think about David and find strength in the LORD your God. He is there for you. He is all the strength you need to get you through. If you are greatly distressed or in serious trouble, may you find strength in the LORD our God. God is our refuge and our strength. He is always ready to help in times of trouble (Psalm 46:1).

Manna Moment

When you need strength connect with Almighty God. Lie on your back, close your eyes and focus on the LORD, the source of all strength and power.

Day 48: His Presence Our Blessing

David was afraid of the LORD that day and said, "How can the ark of the LORD ever come to me?" He was not willing to take the ark of the LORD to be with him in the City of David. Instead, he took it aside to the house of Obed-Edom the Gittite. The ark of the LORD remained in the house of Obed-Edom the Gittite for three months, and the LORD blessed him and his entire household.

2 Samuel 6:9-11 (NIV)

More blessed are we than Obed-Edom. We have the Spirit of the living God dwelling in our hearts just like it dwelled in the ark of the Israelites.

When we accepted Jesus Christ as our Lord and Savior and invited Him into our heart, His Holy Spirit took up residence. Wherever we go, we carry His Spirit with us. We are indeed blessed. Our entire households are also blessed. Enjoy His Presence with you, today.

Manna Moment

What blessings are you experiencing in your life right now? Offer up a shout of thanksgiving.

Day 49: A Life of Desolation

And Tamar took the bread she had prepared and brought it to her brother Amnon in his bedroom. But when she took it to him to eat, he grabbed her and said, "Come to bed with me, my sister." "Don't my brother!" she said to him. "Don't force me. Such a thing should not be done in Israel! Don't do this wicked thing."

But he refused to listen to her, and since he was stronger than she, he raped her.
—2 Samuel 13:10-12, 14 (NIV)

Due to the above incident, 2 Samuel 13:20 reports that Tamar lived in her brother's house as a desolate woman. Even though she was a princess, daughter of King David, her life became one of disgrace and shame. We do not know if she ever recovered from this tragedy.

I ask myself, how many people are living desolate lives, lonely, barren, and fallen lives, while they could be living as princes and princesses of King Jesus? Did some catastrophe occur in your past? Have you allowed it to bind you to a life of quiet desperation? God does not want you to live a life of misery. He wants you to triumph over the deeds of evil and He has given you the power, in the life and death of Jesus Christ. Jesus came to set us free and to give us life abundantly. He desires for us to live lives of victory, in spite of the calamities that come our way. Don't settle for a bleak life of desolation. It is the LORD's will to release you from anything in your past that is hindering you from living a joyful, abundant life.

Manna Moment

Has some horrendous event locked you into living a desolate life? Ask God to help you let it go and walk into a life full of freedom and joy with no shame.

Day 50: Time of Famine

During the reign of David, there was a famine for three successive years; so David sought the face of the LORD.
—2 Samuel 21:1 (NIV)

Famine is basically a lack of what we need for survival. Human beings have physical needs such as: food, water, clothing and shelter. We also have emotional needs, like the need to be loved and appreciated. We need to be in healthy relationships and sharing God's love with others because He created us to be in fellowship with other people. We have a need to feel safe and secure.

On a physical level, the land becomes very dry and hard during times of famine. Land that was once fruitful is now barren. On an emotional level, our hearts can also grow hard and dry. When scarcity exists in our life our hearts may grow bitter and lifeless. Let us remember that God is able to make bitter waters sweet. He is able to bring that which is dead back to life. When there is a shortage in your life may you be like David and seek the face of the LORD. God promises to provide for all of our needs and He is faithful. He gives us enough to sustain us day by day.

Manna Moment

Are you experiencing a famine in your life? Are you lacking something you need to survive and thrive in this world? Seek the face of the LORD. He promises to supply all of our needs.

Day 51: He is ALL We Need

David sang to the LORD the words of this song when the LORD delivered him from the hand of all his enemies and from the hand of Saul. He said: "The LORD is my rock, my fortress and my deliverer; my God is my rock, in whom I take refuge, my shield and the horn of my salvation. He is my stronghold, my refuge and my savior- from violent men you save me. I call to the LORD, who is worthy of praise, and I am saved from my enemies."

—2 Samuel 22:1-4 (NIV)

When we know the LORD and fellowship with Him consistently we have everything we need. According to Colossians 2:9, we have been given fullness in Christ.

He is our rock, a secure and immovable place for us to stand. He is our fortress, a strong safe haven. He is our refuge, a shelter that protects us from danger. He is our deliverer. He delivers us from our enemies. When the evil one sends flaming arrows toward us God is our shield. He sets us free and saves us.

Manna Moment

Think of all the roles God performs in your life. What more do you need?

Day 52: Darkness into Light

You are my lamp, O LORD; the LORD turns my darkness into light.

—2 Samuel 22:29 (NIV)

David sang a song of praise when the LORD delivered him from the hand of all his enemies. According to the above Scripture, which is a small part of the song, the LORD is our lamp. If there is any darkness in us He turns it into light.

The transformation from darkness into light happens when we open the doors of our hearts and invite Him to enter. We must allow Him access to every corner and crevice of our hearts if we want the conversion to be complete.

It is detrimental to keep parts of our heart locked away from the LORD and His light because no good thing inhabits the darkness. Doubt, anxiety, fear, discouragement and depression are prowling about in the darkness, waiting to launch an attack on their next victim. In the light of the LORD we have confidence, peace, and joy, and our faith is strengthened. Praise the LORD! Allow the glorious light of the LORD to shine into your heart today.

Manna Moment

Is there a place of darkness in your heart? Trust it to the LORD and He will fill it with light.

Day 53: Armed with Strength

It is God who arms me with strength and makes my way perfect. He makes my feet like the feet of a deer; he enables me to stand on the heights.
— 2 Samuel 22:33-34 (NIV)

In times of weakness and weariness, God gives us strength. He provides the strength for us to climb mountains. God arms us with the strength to overcome our fears. With each step we are able to go higher as He perfects our ways. The LORD helps us to stand on high peaks, high above the low valleys we so often tread. May you move on to the high places in your life with God leading you each step of the way.

Manna Moment

Think about the obstacles before you, spiritual, emotional, physical or financial. In which areas do you need to be armed with strength? Beseech God to equip you with strength in the areas identified.

Day 54: Covenant of Love

"O LORD, God of Israel, there is no God like you in heaven above or on earth below - you who keep your covenant of love with your servants who continue wholeheartedly in your way."

— 1 Kings 8:23 (NIV)

There is no god like our God. He created the heavens and the earth, by speaking the word and it happened. He is compassionate, forgiving and full of love. We cannot fathom the depth of His love for us. It goes beyond human understanding. The love of God is so deep and so wide nothing can separate us from it.

The apostle, John declares "How great is the love the Father has lavished on us, that we should be called children of God!" (1 John 3:1) He loves us so much He brought us into His family and calls us His sons and daughters. Thank God that no matter what happens in our lives we can always count on His love. God keeps His covenants and His love endures forever.

Manna Moment

Write a letter to God describing what it feels like to be a recipient of His love. Furthermore, tell God how much you love Him. Keep the letter in the pages of your bible and read it periodically.

Day 55: Celebrate the Good Things

So Solomon observed the festival at that time, and all Israel with him – a vast assembly, people from Lebo Hamath to the Wadi of Egypt. They celebrated it before the LORD our God for seven days and seven days more, fourteen days in all. On the following day he sent the people away. They blessed the king and then went home, joyful and glad in heart for all the good things the LORD had done for his servant David and his people Israel.
— 1 Kings 8:65-66 (NIV)

In the passage above, King Solomon and the Israelite people celebrated the dedication of the Temple for seven days and then in accordance with Leviticus 23:36, they celebrated the Feast of Tabernacles for seven days. Let us remember to celebrate all the good things the LORD has done for us. Like Solomon said in Ecclesiastes, there is a time for everything. It is important to take time to celebrate. Fourteen days may not be feasible for you, but choose the amount of time and let it be a time of great rejoicing. Times of celebration are refreshing and they make the heart glad. Taking time to reflect on what the LORD has done in our lives helps us to keep a heartfelt appreciation and an attitude of gratitude.

During these times of celebration families can gather together, fellowship, share a meal, sing praises, dance unto the LORD, give testimonials and offer up thanksgiving to God. When the Israelites came to celebrate their festivals, they always brought an offering to the LORD. Likewise we should always bring something to the LORD. The most important thing we can offer Him is our heart, open to Him and then a shout of praise and thanksgiving. We can honor Him as the only true source of all we have. However you choose to do it, just remember to take the time to celebrate all the good things the LORD has done.

Manna Moment

What good things do you have to celebrate in your life today? Plan a time of celebration and make it happen.

Day 56: Is your Heart being Led Away From the LORD?

The LORD had clearly instructed his people not to intermarry with those nations, because the women they married would lead them to worship their gods. Yet Solomon insisted on loving them anyway. He had seven hundred wives and three hundred concubines. And sure enough, they led his heart away from the LORD.

— 1 Kings 11:2-3 (NLT)

It is a very sad situation when we allow our hearts to be led away from the LORD. We must be sure the things we permit in our lives do not lead our hearts away from the LORD. The things we insist on having in our lives should draw our hearts closer to God and deeper into His Word.

God knows what is best for us. If he clearly instructs us not to do something it is to our benefit to listen. When we feel in our flesh that we have to have something or we have to do something that is not God's will, we need to overcome our flesh and abide by the Holy Spirit who dwells in us. If we do this, we will not fall into any traps the devil has set for us. Our heavenly Father will steer us away from the stumbling blocks, if we only listen. Examine the current condition of your heart. Look at the things and people in your life.

Manna Moment

Is there anything or anyone in your life leading your heart away from the LORD? Remove any obstacles from your life that hinder you from growing closer to the LORD. If it is a relationship you must maintain, then bring it into proper alignment by putting God first. Draw near to the LORD in prayer.

Day 57: God Provides

*"As surely as the Lord your God lives,"
she replied, (the widow at Zarephath) "I
don't have any bread - only a handful of flour
in a jar and a little oil in a jug. I am gathering
a few sticks to take home and make a meal for
myself and my son, that we may eat it - and
die."*
*Elijah said to her, "Don't be afraid. Go
home and do as you have said. But first make
a small cake of bread for me from what you
have and bring it to me, and then make something for yourself and your son."*
— 1 Kings 17:12,13 (NIV)

*She went away and did as Elijah had told her.
So there was food every day for Elijah and
for the woman and her family. For the jar of
flour was not used up and the jug of oil did
not run dry, in keeping with the word of the
LORD spoken by Elijah.*
— 1 Kings 17:15-16 (NIV)

There are times in our lives when the resources we have do not seem like enough. Sometimes it seems like the available funds will not cover the tithe, the bills and the necessities. However, when we are faithful and obedient with our money we get through the month and everything has been covered. God stretches our resources.

At other times it is inner resources we lack. We are sure we do not have the strength we need to get through the latest trial and like the widow, we may feel near death. But when it is all over we look back in amazement at how God brought us through it. There may be times when we may feel we do not have the time to stop tending to our busy schedules to help someone else who is in need. Nevertheless, when we stop and take the time to assist someone else, we find that we still managed to complete the really important stuff. During the process of rearing our children there are days when it seems like we do not have the patience that is needed. However, through the growing years, God manages to gradually increase our patience.

Whether it is physical resources or inner resources, God, in His love and great wisdom does not let us run dry. The widow at Zarephath had to trust in the word of the Lord and she followed through in obedience. As we trust in the Lord and obey His word, God will provide what we need to survive and thrive. He is Jehovah Jireh, God the Provider.

Manna Moment

Think of a time when your resources were scarce. Recall how God provided? Praise the LORD for His provision.

Day 58: Wavering Between Two Opinions

Elijah went before the people and said, "How long will you waver between two opinions? If the LORD is God, follow him; but if Baal is God, follow him." But the people said nothing.
—1 Kings 18:21 (NIV)

We often find ourselves at a crossroads in life, wavering between two opinions, wondering which one to choose. Sometimes the road God asks us to embark upon seems too difficult and we want to take the one that looks easier. We like shortcuts. Do not waver, do not hesitate, pause or ponder.

Follow the LORD our God. His way is the best way. When the time comes choose the LORD, do not be silent.

Manna Moment

Are you wavering between two opinions? Choose to follow the LORD.

Day 59: "I Have Had Enough"

Elijah was afraid and ran for his life. When he came to Beersheba in Judah, he left his servant there, while he himself went a day's journey into the desert. He came to a broom tree, sat down under it and prayed that he might die. "I have had enough, LORD," he said. "Take my life; I am no better than my ancestors." Then he lay down under the tree and fell asleep.

—1 Kings 19:3-5 (NIV)

Are you at the point where you feel like you have had enough? Have you felt faint and weary running around in the hot, dry desert? Here is how Elijah found restoration: First, he rested. He laid down and fell asleep (1 Kings 19:5). Second, he ate a good meal. All at once an angel touched him and said, "Get up and eat" (1 Kings 19:5). So he got up, ate and drank. Strengthened by that food, he traveled forty days and forty nights (1 Kings 19:8). Third, he went to God. He traveled until he reached Horeb, the mountain of God (1 Kings 19:8).

When you feel like you are hanging on by a very thin string, first find rest. Then, take in nourishment. Next, use your strength to seek the presence of God and you will be comforted.

Manna Moment

If you are at the end of your rope, list the factors responsible for your weariness. In Elijah's case it was fear. Take care of your physical body by getting the proper amount of rest and eating well balanced meals. Take care of your spiritual and emotional needs by spending time alone with God. Entreat Him to completely renew you, body, soul and spirit. Instead of hanging on by a string, plant your feet securely on the foundation of Jesus Christ.

Day 60: First Seek Counsel

So he asked Jehoshaphat, "Will you go with me to fight against Ramoth Gilead?" Jehoshaphat replied to the king of Israel, "I am as you are, my people as your people, my horses as your horses." But Jehoshaphat also said to the king of Israel, "First seek the counsel of the LORD."

—1 Kings 22:4-5 (NIV)

Take note of the wisdom exhibited by Jehoshaphat and seek the counsel of the LORD before making any and all decisions. Sometimes we are unaware of the battles others may be trying to draw us into, battles the LORD did not intend for us to fight. Do not allow the pressure of others to force you into making a decision without taking time to seek the LORD.

We are blind to the traps the enemy has set for us, but if we seek His counsel, the LORD will maneuver us around the snares of the devil. He will always lead us and guide us in the right direction, according to His purpose and plan for our lives.

Manna Moment

Consider the risks involved in doing things your own way without consulting the LORD. Ask God to give you the wisdom to seek and follow His guidance everyday.

Day 61: Leaving a Legacy

He did what was pleasing in the LORD's sight, just as his ancestor David had done.
Hezekiah trusted in the LORD, the God of Israel. There was never another king like him in the land of Judah, either before or after his time. He remained faithful to the LORD in everything, and he carefully obeyed all the commands the LORD had given Moses. So the LORD was with him, and Hezekiah was successful in everything he did.
—2 Kings 18:3, 5-7 (NLT)

Have you ever thought about what you would like people to say about you after you have gone to be with the Lord? In this portion of Scripture we have a wonderful account of the legacy Hezekiah left behind. If the goals of our lives are similar to Hezekiah's legacy, our first goal is to do what is pleasing in the LORD's sight. What deep abiding peace we would have in our hearts knowing that everything we did was pleasing in the sight of the LORD.

Our second goal would be to trust in the LORD, completely. Envision trusting in the LORD so much that people say, "There was never another (fill in the blank with what you do) like (insert your name) in the land of (insert where you live) either before or after this time. For example, "There was never another school teacher like Ms. Smith in all of San Diego, either before or after this time."

This is not so we can beat our chest and brag about what we have done. It is so we can take comfort in knowing that we fulfilled our God-given purpose and touched the lives of others in a special way. Whatever God has given you to do, give it your all and you will be the best.

The third goal is to remain faithful to the LORD in everything. This is a call to relinquish every area of your life into the LORD's hands. Living a totally surrendered life will guarantee your success in everything you do.

Manna Moment

Record the legacy you would like to leave behind. What do you consider to be the most significant things for people to remember about you after you have departed this earth to join the Lord in heaven?

Day 62: Spread it Out

After Hezekiah received the letter and read it, he went up to the LORD's Temple and spread it out before the LORD. And Hezekiah prayed this prayer before the LORD: "O LORD, God of Israel, you are enthroned between the mighty cherubim! You alone are God of all the kingdoms of the earth. You alone created the heavens and the earth. Listen to me, O LORD, and hear! Open your eyes, O LORD, and see! Listen to Sennacherib's words of defiance against the living God."

—2 Kings 19:14-16 (NLT)

Do you have circumstances in your life that defy the word of God?

Are you feeling frustrated or stressed out, when Jesus told us that He is leaving us with a gift—peace of mind and heart (John 14:27)? Are you fearful, when God's Word tells us that God has not given us a spirit of fear (2 Timothy 1:2)? Are you tired, when Isaiah 40:31 tells us that those who hope in the LORD will renew their strength? It goes on to say they will run and not grow weary, and they will walk and not be faint.

He alone is God and His Word stands forever. His Word will be around but your circumstances are temporary. Speak the Word into your life. It is a firm foundation you can plant your feet on.

Manna Moment

Write down whatever is contrary to the Word of God in your life. Spread it out before the LORD, pray about it and leave it in His hands.

Day 63: Are You Being Held Captive?

The people of Judah were taken captive to Babylon because of their unfaithfulness.
— 1 Chronicles 9:1 (NIV)

There are different types of captivity. There is a physical captivity, where you are put in actual chains and beaten into a life of submission and servitude, also known as slavery.

However, our minds can be held in captivity. If there is an area of our lives where we are not totally and completely trusting in the LORD, the enemy can hold our minds captive in this area. We can be tortured in our minds with a barrage of worst-case scenarios and "what if" situations. For example, if I don't trust God with my finances, instead of keeping my eyes on Him I will be constantly watching all the worldly indicators for my financial security and my peace will hang in the balance of fluctuating circumstances.

We can also be held captive by our emotions. Take the emotion of fear. Fear can be very debilitating and often keeps us from doing what we know God wants us to do.

Another way we can be stuck in captivity is by some addictive habit, such as smoking or overeating. As long as we struggle with some kind of addiction we are imprisoned.

By allowing the enemy to keep us in bondage we miss out on experiencing the freedom that Jesus provides for us. To gain victory, we have to confess doubt and unbelief to the LORD as sin. Ask God to increase and strengthen your faith in any area where it is weak or nonexistent. Jesus came to set the captives free. Walk in the liberty we have in Christ. We were set free when Jesus was on the cross and declared, "It is finished." Allow Him to cut off your chains and release you from confinement. Live free.

Manna Moment

Are you being held captive in any area of your life? Ask God to grow your faith in this area. And you water it with the Word of God by reading Scriptures that relate to your particular challenge.

Day 64: Seek His Face Always

Give thanks to the LORD, call on his name; make known among the nations what he has done. Sing to him, sing praise to him; tell of all his wonderful acts. Glory in his holy name; let the hearts of those who seek the LORD rejoice. Look to the LORD and his strength; seek his face always.
— 1 Chronicles 16:8-11 (NIV)

Instead of looking at what we can do, lets look to the LORD and His strength. He is the One who spoke the world into existence. God "said" and it was "done." Let us look to the One who put each star in the sky and knows them all by name. Look to the One who sets the sun on its path each day. Give thanks to the Lord and sing praises to Him for all of His wonderful deeds. Rejoice in His Presence. Call on His name and seek His face, continually.

Manna Moment

Imagine the LORD sitting next to your bed when you wake up each morning, with a big smile on His face. The smile is indicative of the LORD's excitement and anticipation of spending time with you. Do not disappoint Him. Seek His face at all times.

Day 65: Fight Bravely by Praying Boldly

"Be courageous! Let us fight bravely to save our people and the cities of our God. May the LORD's will be done."
— 1 Chronicles 19:13 (NLT)

We do not have to fight a physical battle for the LORD like Joab and the Israelite troops. The battle we fight is a spiritual battle. We fight this battle on our knees in prayer. It is a battle against the powers of this dark world and against the spiritual forces of evil in the heavenly realms (Ephesians 6:12).

In prayer we fight for our marriages, our children, our families and our cities to be saved. So take time to pray boldly and with great confidence that your Father in heaven hears your voice and He will answer the call. When you give whatever battles you are fighting to the LORD in prayer you will gain the victory. May the LORD's will be done in your life, in your family, in your home and in your city.

Manna Moment:

What battles are you facing right now? Put them on the LORD's battlefield in prayer.

Day 66: Thank and Praise the LORD

They were also to stand every morning to thank and praise the LORD. They were to do the same in the evening and whenever burnt offerings were presented to the LORD on Sabbaths and at New Moon festivals and at appointed feasts.
— 1 Chronicles 23:30-31 (NIV)

During Old Testament times, the Levites were to stand every morning and evening to thank and praise the LORD. In 1 Peter 2:9, the apostle Peter tells us we are God's chosen people, a royal priesthood and a holy nation. As we seek the LORD each day, may we remember to thank and praise the LORD for all He is doing in our lives. May we thank Him for His goodness. And at the end of each day, let us offer a sacrifice of thanks and praise to the LORD for His faithfulness in getting us through another day.

Manna Moment

Find at least one thing to thank and praise the LORD for in the morning and another thing in the evening.

Day 67: Do the Work

David also said to Solomon his son, "Be strong and courageous, and do the work. Do not be afraid or discouraged, for the LORD God, my God, is with you. He will not fail you or forsake you until all the work for the service of the temple of the LORD is finished."
— 1 Chronicles 28:20 (NIV)

Look at the task the LORD has given to you. What cause has He put on your heart to support? Who is that needy person He has called you to help? Who is that difficult person He has called you to love? Who has hurt you and now God is asking you to forgive them?

May we put all of our hearts into doing the work of the LORD. Do not be afraid or discouraged by the size or the level of difficulty the task requires. If God called you to do it, He will get you through it. The LORD will not fail you, nor forsake you. He is always with you.

Manna Moment

What work is God asking you to do right now? Do the work and God will be faithful to see it to completion.

Day 68: Set Your Heart to Seek the LORD

Those from every tribe of Israel who set their hearts on seeking the LORD, the God of Israel, followed the Levites to Jerusalem to offer sacrifices to the LORD, the God of their fathers.
— 2 Chronicles 11:16 (NIV)

When Rehoboam succeeded his father Solomon as King, Israel became a divided kingdom. King Rehoboam ruled the Southern Kingdom, known as Judah and Jeroboam ruled the Northern Kingdom, called Israel. The Levites throughout Israel abandoned their pasturelands and property to go to Judah (2 Chronicles 11:14). All of the people in Israel who set their hearts on seeking the LORD followed the Levites to Jerusalem.

Have you set your heart to seek the LORD? Are you willing to give up everything you have to seek the LORD? When you awoke this morning and started going down your mental list of things to do, was "seek the LORD" at the top of the list? At the beginning of each day there has to be a conscious decision made in our hearts to seek the LORD. On the other hand, it may be a habit for you to wake up and assume a posture of prayer, seeking the LORD with an open heart. Open in the sense that you are willing to do whatever He directs you to do.

To have the most productive and meaningful day, start by setting your heart to seek the LORD and His will. Acknowledge that this day is not about you. You are here to fulfill the assignment the LORD has for you. Set your will aside and ask God what His will is. Ask Him to direct your steps and put His words in your mouth.

Sometimes what we desire to do with our time is opposed to God's desires. Like the Levites who left the Northern Kingdom, we must be willing to give up *our stuff* or move it further down on our "to do" list.

Manna Moment

If you have not already done so, set your heart to seek the LORD and make this a daily practice.

Day 69: Reliance on the LORD Brings Victory!

The men of Israel were subdued on that occasion, and the men of Judah were victorious because they relied on the LORD, the God of their fathers.
— 2 Chronicles 13:18 (NIV)

This Scripture refers to a war that took place between Abijah, the King of Judah and Jeroboam, the King of Israel. In this battle, Israel had twice as many able troops than Judah (2 Chronicles 13:3). But they did not have the LORD on their side. Instead of losing courage the men of Judah cried out to the LORD and God delivered the men of Israel into their hands. Victory was theirs because they relied on the LORD and not their own power and strength.

As long as we constantly rely on the LORD, we will be victorious. When we look to the LORD in the midst of our difficulties and call on Him, He will make us victorious. When we rely on Him we will not be discouraged by how things appear. Look at Israel with 800,000 men and Judah with only 400,000. The numbers didn't matter, when God was put into the equation.

When things do not look good for you, just keep relying on the LORD and you will be victorious.

Manna Moment

Think of a time when circumstances looked grim. Recall how the LORD brought you through. Thank God for His faithfulness.

Day 70: Be Strong and Do Not Give Up

"But as for you, be strong and do not give up, for your work will be rewarded." When Asa heard these words and the prophecy of

*Azariah son of Oded the prophet, he took
courage.*
—2 Chronicles 15:7-8 (NIV)

These verses of Scripture are part of a prophecy
Azariah, son of Oded the prophet, spoke to Asa, king
of Judah. The words spoken to Asa gave him courage
and he removed the detestable idols from the land
and repaired the altar of the LORD.

The LORD calls us to be strong also, and we will
be rewarded for completing the work He has given
to us. The nature of the labor may vary, whether it is
employment on a job or as a business owner, or the
duties we perform as a parent or spouse. It may be a
volunteer position in the church. All of our assignments matter to our heavenly Father. As we commit
our tasks to the LORD, we are storing up treasures
in heaven and we can take courage knowing that our
efforts will be rewarded. We can be strong because
we have the Holy Spirit living inside of us. God has
not given us a fragile or weak spirit. According to
2 Timothy 1:7, He has given us a spirit of power.
Whatever work He has given you, on this earth, be
strong and do not give up.

Manna Moment

Look at the responsibilities involved in the
different roles you fulfill. Commit the work you
carry out in each role to the LORD. Ask for His help
and strength so you can put your very best into each
task.

Day 71: Fully Committed

For the eyes of the LORD range throughout the earth to strengthen those whose hearts are fully committed to him.
—2 Chronicles 16:9 (NIV)

The LORD is constantly searching for people whose hearts are fully committed to Him, and when He finds them He gives them strength. Are you feeling a little weak? Need strength? Make sure your heart is fully committed to the LORD. A heart that is fully committed to the LORD is always ready and eager to do His will. A heart that is fully committed to the LORD puts all hope and trust in Him regardless of what setbacks may come. Be fully committed to the LORD today.

Manna Moment

Search your heart to see if there is anything hindering you from fully committing to the LORD.

Day 72: Look to God for Help

"And now see what the armies of Ammon, Moab, and Mount Seir are doing. You would not let our ancestors invade those nations when Israel left Egypt, so they went around them and did not destroy them. Now see how they reward us! For they have come to throw us out of your land, which you gave us as

an inheritance. O our God, won't you stop them? We are powerless against this mighty army that is about to attack us. We do not know what to do, but we are looking to you for help."

—2 Chronicles 20:10-12 (NLT)

When you are in a tight situation and you do not know what to do, the best thing to do is to look to God for help. Without His help we are powerless. All of our praise belongs to God, because He is faithful and He comes to our aid when we call on Him. He is our helper.

In response to the above petition of King Jehoshaphat, the LORD told them not to be afraid or discouraged because the battle was not theirs, but God's (2 Chronicles 20:15). According to 2 Chronicles 20:17, the Israelites only had to take their positions, stand still and watch the LORD's victory, because He was with them. Their position was to sing praise to the LORD. When they began to sing and give praise, the LORD caused the armies of Ammon, Moab, and Mount Seir to start fighting among themselves and not a single one of their enemies escaped.

When the creditors threaten, when the children rebel, when friends abandon you, when you are being lied on, verbally attacked, treated unfairly, betrayed or accused, do not be afraid and do not be discouraged. Look to God for help and let Him fight your battle. Whatever happens, continue to give praise and sing to the LORD. He will help you.

Manna Moment

What situation do you face today? Give it to God and take your position of singing to the LORD and praising Him.

Day 73: Pride Leads to Downfall

Uzziah was sixteen when he became king, and he reigned in Jerusalem fifty-two years. His mother was Jecoliah, from Jerusalem. He did what was pleasing in the LORD's sight, just as his father, Amaziah, had done. Uzziah sought God during the days of Zechariah, who instructed him in the fear of God. And as long as the king sought the LORD, God gave him success.

—2 Chronicles 26: 3-5 (NLT)

Success comes from God. If you seek Him first and foremost in your life, He will give you good success. He is El Shaddai, the One who blesses.

In 2 Chronicles 26:16, we find that when Uzziah became powerful, he also became proud, which led to his downfall. After you have started out on the right path and you are doing the things that please the LORD and He gives you power and success, be sure you stay humble. Do not become puffed up with pride and start thinking more highly of yourself than you should. If you do, you will deceive yourself. Remember, pride goes before destruction. It is only by the grace of God that you have what you have and that you are where you are in life. The LORD hates pride, but He gives grace to the humble.

To remain humble before the LORD we must keep Him first in all we do. We should not let other people or the things we have in our lives take precedence over Him. Spouses, children, jobs, TV watching and other recreational activities are a lesser priority. A humble heart acknowledges that God is LORD above and on the earth and continually seeks Him for direction and guidance. A humble person praises the LORD for all He has done, all He is doing and for what He will do in the future.

Manna Moment

Bow down and worship God for who He is and for all He has done in your life. Thank Him for the success that you have in your life right now. Ask Him to help you keep a humble heart.

Day 74: Every Side

So the LORD saved Hezekiah and the people of Jerusalem from the hand of Sennacherib king of Assyria and from the hand of all the others. He took care of them on every side.
—2 Chronicles 32:22 (NIV)

The LORD sent an angel to save Hezekiah and the people of Jerusalem from their enemies. This is the kind of God we serve. He takes care of His people on all sides. There is no part of our lives too complicated or too difficult for the LORD to handle. He not only takes care of us spiritually, but physically and emotionally as well. If we put them in His hands, God takes care of our physical needs, our relationships and our emotions.

Let Him take care of you on every side. Give it all to Him! Once you put something into His hands you must let go and let God work. He covers you in the back, in the front, on the sides and from top to bottom. Hallelujah!

Manna Moment

Do you feel vulnerable to the attacks of the enemy? Draw closer to God. As you dwell in His Presence He protects you on all sides.

Day 75: The Eye of God Watches Over Us

They also asked, "What are the names of the men constructing this building?" But the eye of their God was watching over the elders of the Jews, and they were not stopped until a report could go to Darius and his written reply be received.

—Ezra 5:4-5 (NIV)

Just like the eye of God was watching over the elders of the Jews, the eye of God watches over His people today. He watches over us to keep us moving in the right direction. He keeps watch over us to protect us from the snares of the enemy. He observes us with eyes of love.

El Roi is the God who sees everything. When it seems like no one is concerned about your struggle, God is. He is aware of your anguish and your heartaches. When you hurt, God feels the pain. Please know our God is faithful and you can trust Him one hundred percent to bring you through the setbacks that come your way.

Manna Moment

As you go about your daily tasks, doing what the LORD has given you to do, be mindful that the eye of God is fixed upon you twenty-four hours a day, seven days a week.

Day 76: The Hand of God

"The gracious hand of our God is on everyone who looks to him…"
—Ezra 8:22 (NIV)

Ezra, the priest, spoke these words to the King before him and a group of leaders from Israel took the journey back to Jerusalem. They were in Babylon where they had been exiled. Ezra records that the hand of God was on them and protected them from enemies and bandits along the way (Ezra 8:31). The gracious hand of God will be on you like it was on Ezra and his men.

As you keep your eyes on our heavenly Father, His gracious hand is on you, to guide and protect you. Keep your eyes clearly focused on God, Abba Father, and you will not be disappointed at the work of His hand. When your enemies are hot on your trail the hand of God will cover you. He will protect you from any enemy that rises up against you.

Manna Moment

Do you see God's hand operating in the circumstances of your life? Picture His hand patting you on the back as He cheers you on as a good and faithful servant. Imagine the hand of God on your shoulder as a source of support and strength. Feel His hand as He wipes away your tears and comfort you in times of sadness.

Day 77: God Has Not Deserted Us

Though we are slaves, our God has not deserted us in our bondage. He has shown us kindness in the sight of the kings of Persia: He has granted us new life to rebuild the house of our God and repair its ruins, and he has given us a wall of protection in Judah and Jerusalem.

—Ezra 9:9 (NIV)

Our God is faithful and He does not change. He took care of the Israelites in the times of Ezra and He still takes care of His people today. No matter what you are going through today, God has not deserted you. He shows you His love and His kindness, day by day. He has granted you new life and gives you strength to repair the ruins in your life. God also surrounds His people with a wall of protection.

You may feel abandoned or rejected at times, but God has not deserted you. Like the father of the prodigal son, Jesus holds his arms open wide, always ready to receive you back into fellowship with Him.

Manna Moment

If you have an area in your life that needs repair or rebuilding give it to the Lord in prayer. Close your eyes and imagine what that situation will look like after a touch of the Master's hands gives it new life.

Day 78: When Things Are Not Going Well

They said to me, "Those who survived the exile and are back in the province are in great trouble and disgrace. The wall of Jerusalem is broken down, and its gates have been burned with fire." When I heard these things, I sat down and wept. For some days I mourned and fasted and prayed before the God of heaven."
—Nehemiah 1:3-4 (NIV)

When things are not going well for us, we can follow the actions of Nehemiah. Upon hearing of great trouble, it is likely that we will sit down and weep. When there is trouble in the home we may even feel disgraced. It will seem as though the walls of our home have been torn down. We may enter a time of mourning. Some will engage in a time of fasting but we all need to pray to the God of heaven and earth.

When things are not going well, focus on God who is bigger than any tragedy, problem or circumstance. During challenging times, remember the troubles we experience in this life are light and momentary (2 Corinthians 4:17).

Manna Moment

Are you experiencing difficult times? Lift up your voice to the God of heaven.

Day 79: A Great Project

When word came to Sanballat, Tobiah, Geshem the Arab, and the rest of our enemies that I had rebuilt the wall and not a gap was left in it – though up to that time I had not set the doors in the gates – Sanballat and Geshem sent me this message: "Come, let us meet together in one of the villages on the plain of Ono." But they were scheming to harm me; so I sent messengers to them with this reply: "I am carrying on a great project and cannot go down. Why should the work stop while I leave it and go down to you?"

—Nehemiah 6:1-3 (NIV)

Nehemiah and the rest of the Israelites worked hard from sunrise to sunset rebuilding the wall of Jerusalem. The enemies of the Jewish people opposed the rebuilding of the wall and consistently tried to stop the work. They mocked the children of Israel and threatened to attack them. Sanballat and Geshem sent four messages to Nehemiah in an attempt to stop the work. Each time, Nehemiah replied, "I am carrying on a great project and cannot go down. Why should the work stop while I leave it and go down to you?"

When we are doing what God calls us to, we will often face opposition, some mild, some severe and even violent. We may confront schemes meant to distract us or harm us. Sometimes opposition fires consistently and at other times it is sparse. Whatever the case may be, we ought to stay focused on the task at hand, like Nehemiah. We cannot allow the enemy to distract us from the work of God.

Any work the LORD assigns to us is a great project. If it is raising our children in the admonition of the LORD, walking in love with our spouse, being an honest, reliable business person, or teaching children in Sunday school, God has called us to it and it is a great work. We influence people for the kingdom of God. Those who oppose the work of God will not appreciate our efforts, but God protects us. I encourage you to continue moving forward with the great projects God calls you to.

Manna Moment

What great projects have you been given? In spite of the schemes of the enemy, keep concentrating on your God-given assignments.

Day 80: Joy is Your Strength

Nehemiah said, "Go and enjoy choice food and sweet drinks, and send some to those who have nothing prepared. This day is sacred to our Lord. Do not grieve, for the joy of the LORD is your strength."
                                    —Nehemiah 8:10 (NIV)

King Solomon tells us in Ecclesiastes that there is a time for everything. There is a time to weep and mourn and there is a time to laugh and dance. Weeping may last for the night, but let joy come in the morning. In times of sadness and sorrow lay all of your concerns in the hand of God. Do not be heavily burdened. And may the God of all comfort, fill you with His joy that you may have the strength you need to get you through the day.

When the joy of the LORD runs deep within your soul it is not easily changed by outside circumstances. In, Philippians 4:4, we are directed to rejoice in the Lord always. May His joy bubble over in your heart and touch those who come your way today.

Manna Moment

Philippians 4:4-6 says: Rejoice in the Lord always. I will say it again: Rejoice! Let your gentleness be evident to all. The Lord is near. Do not be anxious about anything, but in everything, by prayer and petition, with thanksgiving, present your requests to God. Meditate on this passage until your spirit and soul bubbles over with joy.

Day 81: A Forgiving God

They refused to listen and failed to remember the miracles you performed among them. They became stiff-necked and in their rebellion appointed a leader in order to return to their slavery. But you are a forgiving God, gracious and compassionate, slow to anger and abounding in love. Therefore you did not desert them,
—Nehemiah 9:17 (NIV)

Whenever you feel you have done something wrong, put a big "But God" after it.

Our God is a forgiving God. Once we confess our sins, we can trust God to forgive us. He is full of grace. Because of God's grace we receive unmerited favor, benefits we did not earn and a kindness we do not deserve. Our God is compassionate. He feels for us and cares about us so deeply. His love for us has no limits or boundaries, which is why He sent His only Son, Jesus Christ, to this earth to reconcile us to Himself. Each of us has much more of God's love than we will ever comprehend with our finite minds. Accept the fact that God loves you (insert your name)! And He forgives you.

Manna Moment

Confess your sins to God daily. If the devil continues to condemn you after you have confessed a sin, say to yourself, "I serve a forgiving God and I am forgiven."

Day 82: For Such a Time as This

When Esther's words were reported to Mordecai, he sent back this answer: "Do not think that because you are in the king's house you alone of all the Jews will escape. For if you remain silent at this time, relief and deliverance for the Jews will arise from another place, but you and your father's family will perish. And who knows but that you have come to royal position for such a time as this?"
—Esther 4:12-14 (NIV)

A plot had been set into motion to destroy all the Jews. Haman, an enemy of the Jews, sought and received permission from King Xerxes to issue an order to destroy, kill and annihilate all the Jews (Esther 3:8-13). In the above scripture, Mordecai, Queen Esther's cousin is persuading her to risk her life and speak to the king on behalf of the Jewish people. After three days of fasting and praying, Queen Esther approached the King and interceded on behalf of the Jews and as a result her people were saved from total destruction.

God had Queen Esther in the right place at the right time to bring about His plan. Likewise, God has us on this earth at this time to fulfill the plans He has for these times we are living right now. He wants us to make a difference in this dark and depraved world. There are hurting and lost people in our sphere of influence who need the light, love and hope only we can share with them. They need to know the God of the universe. Reach out and make a difference in your world. We are here for such a time as this.

Manna Moment

Consider which role God has for you to play for such a time as this? What steps can you take today to move you in that direction? Commit to doing what you are able to do each day and you will experience success.

Day 83: Praise His Name

He said, "I came naked from my mother's womb, and I will be stripped of everything when I die. The LORD gave me everything I had, and the LORD has taken it away. Praise the name of the LORD!" In all of this, Job did not sin by blaming God.

—Job 1:21-22 (NLT)

Job had just been notified that his oxen and donkeys had been raided, his farmhands killed, his sheep and shepherds burned up, his camels stolen, his servants killed and all his children were dead. Job's response to learning he had lost everything but his wife and the house he lived in was to tear his robe in grief, shave his head and fall to the ground before God and give Him praise.

When we think of people who have experienced a great deal of suffering Job's name always comes up. How often do we respond to suffering and trials like Job? Yet very few people have known the depth of loss and suffering that Job went through. Even after all of this, Job greatly suffered in his physical body and lived with a wife who did not have a supportive attitude. Perhaps we need to acquaint ourselves to the reality that the LORD has given us everything we have and He can take it away. Job asked his wife, "Should we accept only good things from the hand of God and never anything bad?"

In spite of all the suffering and loss, Job's story concludes on a very positive note. At the end of all Job's suffering, God gave him double for his trouble. God restored his fortunes, twice as much as he had before his troubles began. Job also had seven more sons and three more daughters.

Manna Moment

The next time you find yourself in the midst of a trial, remember Job's testimony, and praise the name of the LORD!

Day 84: What I Feared

"What I feared has come upon me, what I dreaded has happened to me. I have no peace, no quietness; I have no rest, but only turmoil."

—Job 3:25-26 (NIV)

Have you ever wondered why Job feared and dreaded when God had blessed him so much? According to Job 1:10, God kept a hedge around Job, his household and everything he owned. He also blessed the work of his hands.

Do you realize how much God has blessed us? He puts a hedge of protection around us and blesses the work of our hands, but we also find ourselves experiencing fear of some kind. It may be a natural part of the human experience to fear and dread. What do you fear? Is there something you dread or something that causes you great anxiety? Thank God that most of what we fear never comes to pass. Remember perfect love drives out fear (1 John 4:18). God's love is perfect and He pours His love on us everyday. So receive the love of God in your heart and release all fear to Him.

Some of us can relate to Job when he says he has no peace and quiet, no rest, only turmoil. We all have days we feel we just need rest. That is why Jesus tells all those who are heavily burdened to come to Him. He gives us peace and His will for us is that we are anxious for nothing. Enter into His rest today, emotionally, spiritually and physically. May the peace of our Lord Jesus Christ be with you.

Manna Moment

Meditate on the perfect love of God. It will drive out all fear.

Day 85: In His Hand

In His hand is the life of every creature and the breath of all mankind.
—Job 12:10 (NIV)

It is as the old song goes: "He's got the whole world in His hands." The life of every living being is in the hand of Almighty God. Every breath we take is in the hands of the One who laid the foundation of the earth and set the sun on its path. He established the limits of the oceans and placed the moon and stars in position. Surely, He can handle the various challenges we face in this life. Have no fear and be at peace for your life is in His hand.

Manna Moment

Picture the big hand of God holding you in the palm of His hand. Notice how calm and relaxed your body becomes as you realize God has everything in control.

Day 86: Our Advocate Is on High

Even now my witness is in heaven; my advocate is on high. My intercessor is my friend as my eyes pour out tears to God; on behalf of a man he pleads with God as a man pleads for his friend.

—Job 16:19-21 (NIV)

In the midst of his unbearable pain and suffering, Job looked for Someone to intercede on his behalf. Whether we are floundering in extreme agony or soaring on the heights of euphoria, we can be comforted with the knowledge that our Advocate, Jesus Christ, is on high. As Satan accuses us before our God day and night (Revelation 12:10), Jesus pleads our case with the Father. We always have Someone on our side. We have a Friend who laid down His life for us and whose precious blood washes away our sins. Our advocate is on high.

Manna Moment

Is the devil convicting you about a sin you have already confessed? Close your eyes and picture yourself sitting in a court of law, giving your file to your lawyer who is Jesus Christ. Visualize Him turning to His Father and saying, "It is all taken care of. My blood has wiped all my child's sins away." Imagine hearing the voice of our heavenly Father saying, "Not guilty. You are free to go. Court adjourned."

Day 87: Move Onward and Forward

The righteous will move onward and forward, and those with pure hearts will become stronger and stronger.

—Job 17:9 (NLT)

We all have a purpose in this life. We have a call on our lives, a course to complete, a race to run, battles to fight and mountains to climb. It is not a test for speed, but one of endurance and perseverance. As children of God we are called to move forward. There will be times when God wants us to stand still, but in the whole scheme of life we have to make progress if we are to fulfill the mission our heavenly Father has given to each one of us.

Sometimes the forward motion will be by leaps and bounds and at other times it may be inch by inch, but as long as we are moving forward we will eventually reach our destination. May you grow stronger and stronger as you move onward and forward in this life.

Manna Moment

What is your next step toward your destination? If you do not know, pray and ask God to reveal it to you.

Day 88: Follow His Steps

My feet have closely followed his steps; I have kept to his way without turning aside. I have not departed from the commands of his lips; I have treasured the words of his mouth more than my daily bread.
                              —Job 23:11-12 (NIV)

In the first chapter of Job, God describes Him as a blameless and upright man. Following the steps of the LORD and treasuring the words of His mouth were habits that guaranteed Job stayed on the right course.

To ensure our well being, we also need to follow the steps of the LORD closely, without turning to the left or the right. The second we choose to go a different way, marks the beginning of our downfall. In addition, we must treasure His words more than we desire to satisfy our hunger.

Manna Moment

Have you taken steps that went in a different direction from those of the LORD? Get back in step with the LORD and follow His steps closely.

Day 89: Crowned with Glory

When I consider your heavens, the work of your fingers, the moon and the stars which you have set in place, what is man that you

*are mindful of him, the son of man that you
care for him? You made him a little lower
than the heavenly beings and crowned him
with glory and honor.*

—Psalm 8:3-5 (NIV)

Who are human beings that God should think of us? God is the Creator of the universe. According to Isaiah 40:22, we are like grasshoppers to Him. Yet, God formed the earth for us to inhabit. He takes the time to stay intimately acquainted with each one of us. God knows the number of hairs on your head. He bottles up your tears. His ear is always open to hear your cry. Praise the LORD for His constant concern.

We are children of the King, created in His image. He crowns us with glory and honor. Lift your head and let the beauty of our LORD shine upon you. Let us walk with our heads up and our shoulders back, proud to be heirs of God and co-heirs with Christ. If we endure, we shall reign with Jesus (2 Timothy 2:12).

Manna Moment

Imagine the very hands of God setting a crown of glory and honor on your head. What do you say to Him? What feelings are aroused in you?

Day 90: My Cup Overflows

*LORD, you have assigned me my portion and
my cup; you have made my lot secure.*
—Psalm 16:5 (NIV)

Are you trying to get through your day with an empty cup? The LORD has given us a spiritual cup. When we spend time with Him, and in His Word, He fills our cup with the good things we need to get through our day: peace, love, joy, kindness, and patience. Then when we start feeling a little frustrated, anxious or angry, we can pick up our cup and drink in the peace we need to carry on. When we are weak and thirsty we can lift our cup up and take in the spiritual nourishment we need. When our cup is empty it can be filled with undesirable things like loneliness, fear, anxiety, frustration, or unforgiveness.

Make it your first priority to talk to the LORD like He is your best friend and to listen for His still small voice as He speaks to you. May you receive a fresh filling of His Holy Spirit each new day. Then the word in Psalm 23:5 will become a reality in your life and you can say, "My cup overflows." And when your cup overflows there will be plenty to share with others. What a blessing!

Manna Moment

Sit at the LORD's table every day and fill your cup.

Day 91: May All Your Plans Succeed

May the LORD answer you when you are in distress; may the name of the God of Jacob protect you. May he send you help from the sanctuary and grant you support from Zion. May he remember all your sacrifices and accept your burnt offerings. May he give you the desire of your heart and make all your plans succeed.

—Psalm 20:1-5 (NIV

The LORD is worthy of all our praise. He answers us when we are distressed. He protects us. He sends us help and support. The LORD remembers all of our sacrifices and accepts our burnt offerings, burnt because they have borne the flames of adversity.

He will give you the desire of your heart and pleasant success, as your actions line up with His will. Hallelujah!

Manna Moment

Picture God putting the pen in your hand to write the rest of your life story. What would you write? Put it on paper and petition the LORD to give you the desire of your heart.

Day 92: He Answers

Now I now that the LORD saves his anointed; he answers him from his holy heaven with the saving power of his right hand. Some trust in chariots and some in horses, but we trust in the name of the LORD our God.

—Psalm 20:6-7 (NIV)

When you call upon the name of the LORD, He answers from His holy heaven. How does He answer? Sometimes He says *Yes.* Sometimes He says *No.* Sometimes He says *Not right now.* There are times when He answers you through His Word, and there are times when He speaks through other people. At other times God speaks directly to your heart.

Your ears have to be attuned to hear His loving voice. Believe in your heart that God is working for your good, even when you get an answer you were not expecting.

Manna Moment

What questions plague your mind? What pressing problems do you need a solution for? Seek the LORD for the answer. Ask Him to open your ears to hear His reply.

Day 93: Walking Through

Even though I walk through the valley of the shadow of death, I will fear no evil, for you are with me; your rod and your staff, they comfort me.

—Psalm 23:4 (NIV)

Even though we walk through the darkest of valleys, the good news is that we can keep walking. We do not have to stay in the valley and build a house to live in.

If we continually take one step after another, no matter how difficult, we will eventually come out on the other side of the valley. We proceed through the desolate valley of fear and doubt. We pass through the gloomy valley of loneliness and weariness. We travel through the dismal valley of hopelessness and frustration. We progress through the tough valley of anger and resentment. As we move through each valley, we fear no evil because God guides us along on the path with His rod and His staff. They reassure us of His Presence and His guidance.

Manna Moment

What valley are you in? How long have you been there? Move forward confidently, knowing the LORD is your traveling companion.

Day 94: Loving and Faithful Ways

Good and upright is the LORD; therefore he instructs sinners in his ways. He guides the humble in what is right and teaches them his way. All the ways of the LORD are loving and faithful for those who keep the demands of his covenant.

—Psalm 25:8-10 (NIV)

The LORD is good and He does what is right. When we follow the LORD's commands, we are walking in His loving ways and trusting in His faithfulness. Why would we wander away from His lovingkindness and faithfulness? Do we dare think we know a better way? May we humble ourselves and allow the LORD to teach us His way, which is the higher and better way. His way leads to life and success. Walk on the path of the LORD and enjoy the security and comfort of His wonderful love in the process. Rest assured that the LORD will do everything His Word says He will do.

Manna Moment

What keeps you from following the ways of the LORD? Lay it down at the altar of the LORD and surrender to His loving and faithful ways.

Day 95: Our Light

The LORD is my light and my salvation – whom shall I fear?
—Psalm 27:1 (NIV)

The dictionary defines light as "a visible radiant energy." We can see God in us. His light is visible. His light shines and glows on the inside of us. With His energy inside of us we have the power to do things in God's strength, not our own.

What happens in the darkness? You feel all alone in the dark, because you cannot see the others who are in there with you. Darkness brings depression and low energy flow. It is hard to find your way in the darkness. Darkness cripples you and makes you ineffective.

Thank God that when His light comes into our hearts it chases the darkness away. In His light, we can see the path on which we need to walk and the obstacles we need to maneuver around. In His light we can see things clearly. God is light and there is no darkness in Him at all (1 John 1:5). Walk in the light and let your light shine on those around you who may be groping in the darkness.

Manna Moment

Do you feel like you are stumbling around in the dark? Call on God, who turns our darkness into light.

Day 96: Strength and Peace

The LORD gives strength to his people; the LORD blesses his people with peace.
—Psalm 29:11 (NIV)

It is the LORD who gives us strength to rise up out of bed each morning. The LORD gives us strength to persevere through the painful trials and overcome all obstacles. If you need an extra dose of strength today, ask Him for it. He will give it to you.

May you experience the peace of the LORD deep down in your soul. Let His peace wash over your mind and settle on your heart. Allow His peace to comfort you when you lay your head on your pillow at night.

Manna Moment

Are you running low on strength? Are you lacking in the peace department? Solicit the LORD for strength and peace.

Day 97: Favor for a Lifetime

Sing to the LORD, you saints of his; praise his holy name. For his anger lasts only a moment, but his favor lasts a lifetime; weeping may remain for a night but rejoicing comes in the morning.

—Psalm 30:4-5 (NIV)

Praise the LORD! Take joy in knowing that we have the favor of God all the days of our lives. It is not here today and gone tomorrow. This is good news. There will be times of weeping, but there will also be times of great rejoicing.

With His favor we are blessed beyond measure. The favor of God opens doors that were previously shut and locked. It removes obstacles and heals sick bodies. The favor of God turns a "no" into a "yes" and the impossible becomes the possible. This does give us something to sing about!

Manna Moment

Even if you cried yourself to sleep last night, make a choice to rejoice this morning. Praise God for His favor.

Day 98: Never Lack

The lions may grow weak and hungry, but those who seek the LORD lack no good thing.
— Psalm 34:10 (NIV)

What a beautiful promise the above Scripture contains. If we seek the LORD we will not lack any good thing. If we are lacking a good thing we should examine ourselves and see if we truly seek the LORD with all of our hearts and minds. Is there some area of your life where you depend on something or someone else instead of God? Do you put more trust in your job and your boss for your financial security than you do your God? Do you have more trust in a man to be your protector and your shield rather than God? Do certain fears keep you from stepping out in faith and trusting the LORD with everything?

Put all of your trust in the LORD. Trust Him with your relationships. Rely on Him for your finances. Trust Him for your emotional well being, your physical health and your mental health. When we thoroughly seek Him as the source of all we need He will fulfill His Word and we will lack no good thing.

Manna Moment

What are the good things the LORD has provided for you? Are any good things missing from your life? Seek the LORD.

Day 99: Many Troubles

The righteous face many troubles, but the LORD rescues them from each and every one.

—Psalm 34:19 (NLT)

This is a very comforting word we can meditate on whenever trials or troubles come our way. No matter what kind of troubles you face today, no matter how bitter, how frustrating, how challenging the LORD will rescue you from them. No matter how many troubles are staring you in the face today, whether it is one or several, He will deliver you from them all, each and every one. He may allow troubles in our lives for a season to accomplish some higher purpose, to make us better, stronger, or increase our faith, but He will deliver us at His appointed time. Give praise to the LORD for His faithfulness.

Manna Moment

What troubles are you facing today? List them out on a piece of paper; give them to the LORD in prayer. Thank the LORD that He is faithful and He will rescue you from all your troubles.

Day 100: Take Refuge and Drink

How priceless is your unfailing love! Both high and low among men find refuge in the shadow of your wings. They feast on the abundance of your house; you give them drink from your river of delights. For with you is the fountain of life; in your light we see light.

—Psalm 36:7-9 (NIV)

Take refuge in the shadow of God's wings. He is a safe haven for all of humanity.

Drink from His fountain of life until you are absolutely full, for there is overflowing abundance in His house. Take pleasure in drinking from the gushing river of His divine delights: light-hearted laughter, enduring love, calming peace, bubbling joy, absolute forgiveness, complete healing, compassionate understanding, warm comfort, strong protection, rest, mercy, grace, hope, open acceptance, and so on.

Manna Moment

What can you add to the list of God's delights? How often do you drink from the river of His delights?

Day 101: Cultivate Faithfulness

Trust in the LORD, and do good; dwell in the land and cultivate faithfulness. Delight your-

self in the LORD; And He will give you the
desires of your heart.
— Psalm 37:3-4 (NAS)

We are to be people who cultivate faithfulness. We want to do whatever we can to foster the growth of faithfulness in our land. If we had a plant we would make sure it was in good soil with plenty of nutrients, that it got exposure to the sun, and that it was kept at the ideal temperature.

Cultivating faithfulness is similar to taking care of a plant. You are to make sure your heart and mind are taking in the proper nourishment, which is the Word of God. In order to grow, you need exposure to the Son, Jesus Christ. And as a follower of Christ, your ideal temperature is hot. We are to be on fire for the Lord. In the book of Revelation, Jesus told the Church in Laodicea, He does not want lukewarm believers. Once we have trusted in the Lord and received of His goodness, we are moved to do good which in turn promotes the growth of faithfulness in our homes, on our jobs and in our land.

Manna Moment

What seeds can you plant today to encourage faithfulness? Challenge yourself to see how many seeds you can plant and nurture.

Day 102: Make Each Day Count

"Show me, O LORD, my life's end and the number of my days; let me know how fleeting is my life. You have made my days a mere handbreadth; the span of my years is as nothing before you. Each man's life is but a breath.

—Psalm 39:4-5 (NIV)

Each person has a limited number of days to enjoy life on this earth. Let us not take one minute for granted. James 4:14 says we are a mist that appears for a little while and then vanishes. Make a decision that today is the best day of the rest of your life. We cannot change the past, but we can choose now to laugh, love and live for today.

Do not push the pause button on your life in anticipation of some future event. It is okay to stop and fantasize about the future, but do not forget to press play and turn those dreams into reality by fully engaging in the activities of your choosing. Live the life out of every minute God gives you on this side of Heaven. Treasure each second and make each day count.

Manna Moment

Have you been putting off something you always wanted to do? Begin today to actively pursue the desires God has placed in your heart. Live the abundant life of freedom and truth, leaving no regrets behind.

Day 103: Stuck in the Mud and Mire

I waited patiently for the LORD; he turned to me and heard my cry. He lifted me out of the slimy pit, out of the mud and mire; he set my feet on a rock and gave me a firm place to stand.

—Psalm 40:1-2 (NIV)

Have you ever been stuck in the mud? Not only is it dirty but it also has a tendency to stick to you and pull you down, much like the muck and mire of life.

During our walk on the road of life we may step into a puddle of mud or fall into a slimy pit. At some point on our journey, we are subject to find ourselves in the lonely, dark and gloomy pit of depression. Or we may be in the pit of despair where all feels hopeless and useless. At other times we find ourselves in the bone chilling, gut wrenching pit of fear and anxiety. Depression, loneliness, despair, fear, anxiety, weariness and bitterness are all elements of the muck and mire of life.

Once one of them gets a grip on you it does not want to let you go. In fact, instead of rising above the muck, we often find ourselves sinking deeper and deeper. At these times we need to cry out to the LORD and wait patiently for Him. God will turn toward us and lift us up out of our slimy pit. Give

Him your hand and allow Him to pull you out. He will give you solid ground to stand on.

Manna Moment

If you feel stuck in a slimy pit or caught up in the mud and mire of life, ask God to lift you out. Meditate on the following verse as you patiently wait for the LORD to deliver you. Psalm 130:5 says "I wait for the LORD, my soul waits, and in his word I put my hope."

Day 104: Many Thoughts Toward Us

Many, O LORD my God, are the wonders which Thou hast done, and Thy thoughts toward us; There is none to compare with Thee; If I would declare and speak of them, they would be too numerous to count.
—Psalm 40:5 (NAS)

The LORD has so many thoughts toward us and wonders which He has done we cannot count them all. Before we were born, He thought of us and formed us in our mother's womb. He recorded all of our days before one of them came to be. His thoughts of us are so frequent He knows how many hairs we have on our head at any given time. The various thoughts God has about you are indicative of the great love He has for you. Likewise, let your thoughts of Him be too numerous to count.

Manna Moment

Make a special effort to think of the LORD as often as you can throughout the day. Thank Him for all the little things as you go about your day. Think of His greatness and all His works.

Day 105: He Is Our Helper

But may all who search for you be filled with joy and gladness. May those who love your salvation repeatedly shout, "The LORD is great!" As for me, I am poor and needy, but the Lord is thinking about me right now. You are my helper and my savior. Do not delay, O my God.

—Psalm 40:16-17 (NLT)

The LORD is great! He didn't just create us and leave us. He created us and He continues to think about each one of us. He is thinking about you right now. He is not only our Creator, He is also our Savior. He wants to help us.

Manna Moment

Would you like some help from the LORD today? Call on Him.

Day 106: My Joy and My Delight

Send forth your light and your truth, let them guide me; let them bring me to your holy mountain, to the place where you dwell. Then will I go to the altar of God, to God, my joy and my delight. I will praise you with the harp, O God, my God.

—Psalm 43:3-4 (NIV)

Use the Word of truth, to show you the way you should go. Follow the light of the LORD and it will lead you to the place where the presence of the LORD dwells. In His dwelling place, there is an endless supply of love, everlasting joy and deep, abiding peace. He is the source of all we need. There is no lack on His holy mountain. Go to the altar of God and receive all that He has for you. May God be the source of all your joy.

Manna Moment

Delight yourself in the presence of God. Sing your favorite song of praise to the LORD.

Day 107: Be Still

"Be still, and know that I am God; I will be exalted among the nations, I will be exalted in the earth."

—Psalm 46:10 (NIV)

When we are still and direct our attention toward God, we come to know who He is. We become unmistakably aware of how much He deserves all our praise, admiration and honor. During our quiet times with the Father, our minds must be still as well as our bodies. Let us give our minds a rest from the day to day business and focus on the Creator of the universe, in all of His power and glory. In our stillness, knowledge of God wells up inside of us and we sense His loving, gentle Presence.

In His Presence we experience pure joy, our souls grow calm and our spirits are refreshed. When we step out of the whirlwind of our lives we become aware of all He has created for us and we can truly appreciate Him. Be still and know that He is God. There is no other.

Manna Moment

Sit back in your favorite chair and take a moment to unwind. Be still before God and take pleasure in His Presence. After a time of stillness and silence, exalt His name.

Day 108: He Hears My Voice

But I call to God, and the LORD saves me. Evening, morning and noon I cry out in distress, and he hears my voice.
                    —Psalm 55:16-17 (NIV)

Call out to God and He will save you from your troubles. The time of day is irrelevant. His ear is open to hear your voice twenty-four hours a day. He does not sleep or slumber. God is never too busy. If you take the time to call, He is always there to listen.

Shout out in the midst of distress or utter a whisper out of weariness. Cry out in absolute anguish or whimper in pain. If all you can get out is a groan or a "Help me, LORD!" He hears your voice.

Manna Moment

Are you in distress? Lift your voice up to the LORD in the morning, at midday and at night.

Day 109: On Your Side

You keep track of all my sorrows. You have collected all my tears in your bottle. You have recorded each one in your book. On the very day I call to you for help, my enemies will retreat. This I know: God is on my side.
—Psalm 56:8-9 (NLT)

Now here is something to rejoice about: God is on your side. You have the Creator of the universe working on your behalf. In spite of the sorrows you go through, He is working all things together for good in your life. All power and authority belong to Him. Who can fight against the LORD? Victory and success are with Him.

Praise God and remember He is on your side.

Manna Moment

Call to the LORD for help. Rejoice in advance for the upcoming victory.

Day 110: God Fulfills His Purpose

I cry out to God Most High, to God, who fulfills his purpose for me.
—Psalm 57:2 (NIV)

We can be confident that no matter what comes our way God will fulfill His purpose in our lives. He created each one of us with a purpose in mind. Do not believe the enemy when adverse circumstances come and he tries to get you to lose hope and become discouraged. The Word of the Lord prevails over Satan and any of his schemes and the Word of the Lord is that God will fulfill His purpose for you.

Even if we messed up the first time around, we serve a God of second and third chances. When the children of Israel doubted God and refused to enter the Promised Land upon leaving Egypt, God gave them another chance to fulfill His purpose for them. After forty years of wandering in the desert, the Israelites entered their Promised Land and God's purpose for them was fulfilled. God will fulfill His purpose for you as well.

Manna Moment

Take a tablet and write down all the purposes you know God has for you to fulfill. If you are not sure, think about the desires of your heart. What are you passionate about? Seek God's direction for the steps you need to take and His timing on when to take them. When He reveals a step to you, write it down and take the action required to complete it.

Day 111: A Place of Abundance

We went through fire and water, but you brought us to a place of abundance.
—Psalm 66:12 (NIV)

God preserves our lives. Even though we go through the fire of adversity, we are not burned. Even though we go through floodwaters, we do not drown. God brings us to a place of abundant joy, peace and calmness. He brings us to a place of abundant love. Praise the LORD!

Manna Moment

What would you like to have an abundance of in your life? Thank God for the abundance you already have.

Day 112: Provision

*You sent abundant rain, O God, to refresh
the weary Promised Land. There your people
finally settled, and with a bountiful harvest,
O God, you provided for your needy people.*
— Psalm 68:9-10 (NLT)

Just like God provided for His people in their
Promised Land, God will provide for us in our promised land, the destination He has for us. Consider that
wherever you are today is where God wants you to
be and that is where He will provide. He knows the
journey each of us will make in this life and He will
provide for us each step of the way.

We are all needy people. He rains down His Holy
Spirit upon us to refresh us and give us strength. And
His Holy Spirit produces fruit in our lives: love, joy,
peace, patience, kindness, goodness, faithfulness,
gentleness and self-control (Galatians 5:22). May
you enjoy the fruit of a bountiful harvest. The harvest
God works into our lives is generously given and it
produces many rewards in our lives and in the lives
of those around us.

Manna Moment

In what ways do you need God's provision?
Present your needs to God.

Day 113: Restore My Life

Your righteousness reaches to the skies, O God, you who have done great things. Who, O God, is like you? Though you have made me see troubles, many and bitter, you will restore my life again; from the depths of the earth you will again bring me up.
— Psalm 71:19-20 (NIV)

The troubles we see in this life will be many and some will be very bitter, but we have the hope that God will bring restoration to our lives. Though we experience troubles, our God is a God of restoration. He will take those dead areas of your life and heart and breathe resurrection life into them. After God's restoration they will be vibrant. He will take the broken areas (broken relationships, broken finances, for example.) and repair them.

The troubles we see before us today will soon be gone. When God's restoration project is complete you will be whole and healed.

Manna Moment

What relationships or areas in your life need restoring? Do you know someone who needs restoration? Ask God to restore you and the other person.

Day 114: Always with You

Yet I am always with you; you hold me by my right hand. You guide me with your counsel, and afterward you will take me into glory. Whom have I in heaven but you? And earth has nothing I desire besides you.
—Psalm 73:23-25 (NIV)

Let your soul rest peace, knowing that wherever you go and whatever you do our mighty God is always with you. He is with you through thick and thin, at the beginning of each new day and through the night. He holds us by the hand and He leads us toward a glorious destiny. Let your desire be for Him. Seek Him first. May you enjoy the constant companionship of our heavenly Father always.

Manna Moment

How do you experience the presence of God in your day-to-day living? Make it your intention to be aware of His presence throughout your day as much as possible.

Day 115: Our Great Creator

It was you who opened up springs and streams; you dried up the ever flowing rivers. The day is yours and yours also the night; you established the sun and moon. It was you

*who set all the boundaries of the earth; you
made both summer and winter.*
                                    —Psalm 74:15-17 (NIV)

When we reflect on the works of our mighty
God, we stand deeply humbled and in total awe of
His immense power. All power and might belong to
our God. He is Elohim, the Great Creator. He is the
Master. We see His beauty and perfection in all His
works. Everything was created and is held together
in a perfect balance because of Him and His will. He
is magnificent!

The day and the night belong to Him. He is in
control of everything that happens to us, day or night,
in summer or winter. He creates our lives as well as
the world around us. Wow! How can we compete
with a God like Him? Why would anyone try to
compete with God? He is in control even though we
sometimes like to think we are in control.

Manna Moment

Say this prayer to let go and let God.

"Heavenly Father and Creator of the universe,
please help me to let go of the reigns, get out of the
driver's seat and stop fighting against your will. Help
me to relax and go with the flow of Your Holy Spirit
working within me to bring about Your perfect will
in my life and in the world. Please help me, Abba
Father, to face the challenges You have allowed in my
life by embracing You, Your power, Your strength

and Your wisdom. In the name of Jesus Christ I pray. Amen."

Day 116: In the House of God

Better is one day in your courts than a thousand elsewhere; I would rather be a doorkeeper in the house of my God than dwell in the tents of the wicked.
—Psalm 84:10 (NIV)

It is good to dwell in the house of our God. His salvation provides the strong foundation. Accepting Jesus Christ is the key to opening the door to God's house. When you walk through the doors, blessings sweep over you and all your burdens are lifted off of your shoulders. In His house joy abounds and the fragrance of His love permeates every room. Peace adorns the walls of His sanctuary. His glory shines brightly and illuminates His house.

Manna Moment

Imagine yourself in the very dwelling place of God. Do you see the glory that surrounds Him? Can you sense His mighty power and His great love?

Day 117: Our Sun and Shield

For the LORD God is a sun and shield; the LORD bestows favor and honor; no good thing does he withhold from those whose walk

is blameless. O LORD Almighty, blessed is the man who trusts in you.
— Psalm 84:11-12 (NIV)

The LORD God is our sun. He changes our darkness into light. His light shines and shows us the way we should go. The radiance of His light warms and soothes our wounded and weary hearts.

The LORD God is our shield. He protects us from the wiles of our enemy who comes to steal, kill and destroy. He guards us from those who want to harm us. Blessed is the person who trusts in God!

Manna Moment

How has the Lord illuminated your life? Count all the ways.

Day 118: Compassion and Grace

But you, O Lord, are a compassionate and gracious God, slow to anger, abounding in love and faithfulness.
— Psalm 86:15 (NIV)

Thank God for the compassion and grace He gives us every day. Isaiah 30:18 tells us He rises to show us compassion. His empathy reaches out to us no matter what emotional state or circumstance we are in. If you are apprehensive, distressed, lonely, or grieving God understands. He cares so deeply and passionately for us, He fully supplies all the love we need in abundance.

God longs to be gracious to us. When we admit our helplessness to God His grace is there to help us in our time of need. And He is faithful to be there whenever we need Him, which is always. May we continuously feed on the wonderful grace of God.

Manna Moment

Strive to have the same compassion and grace for others that God has for you. Think of a person you can extend God's compassion and grace to and carry it out.

Day 119: My Place of Safety

Those who live in the shelter of the Most High will find rest in the shadow of the Almighty. This I declare of the LORD: He alone is my refuge, my place of safety; He is my God, and I am trusting Him.
                            —Psalm 91:1-2 (NLT)

God alone is our refuge and our place of safety. We will not find safety in our jobs or in the amount of money we earn. Safety is not found in the country we live in or in its existing government. Gated communities and homes with alarms do not guarantee our security.

God alone is our refuge and our place of safety. We can live in His shelter and rest in His shadow. In the shelter of the Most High God we are safe from all the enemy brings our way because He is our armor and our protection. God will shield you with His wings and shelter you with His feathers (Psalm 91:4 NLT).

Manna Moment

How often do you feel vulnerable and insecure? As often as these feelings arise, say the words: "I live in the shelter of the Most High and He is my place of safety."

Day 120: "I'm Slipping!"

I cried out, "I'm slipping!" and your unfailing love, O LORD supported me. When doubts filled my mind, your comfort gave me renewed hope and cheer.
—Psalm 94:18-19 (NLT)

When you lose your balance in life and you are about to slip and fall, cry out to the LORD and His love will support you. His unfailing love will hold you up. When doubt enters your mind, focus on the LORD. Call on Him and He will renew your hope and fill your heart with joy. He will comfort you in His everlasting arms.

Manna Moment

Have you ever slipped into a depressive mode? How did the love of the LORD pick you up?

Day 121: Bow Down

Come, let us bow down in worship, let us kneel before the LORD our Maker; for he is our God and we are the people of his pasture, the flock under his care.

—Psalm 95:6-7 (NIV)

The Lord is our Maker. He formed us while we were in our mother's womb and He knows us better than we know ourselves. The Lord is our God. Our God is living and compassionate. Our God is forgiving and righteous. Our God is mighty. We are the people of His pasture and He knows each one of us by name. We are the flock under His care and He pays special attention to every single one. We are in the safest place of all, in His care. He takes care of our every need.

Manna Moment

Bow down and worship the LORD.

Day 122: The Sheep of His Pasture

Shout for joy to the LORD, all the earth. Worship the LORD with gladness; come before him with joyful songs. Know that the LORD is God, it is he who made us, and we are his; we are his people, the sheep of his pasture.

—Psalm 100:1-3 (NIV)

God made us from the inside out, therefore, we belong to Him. Our hearts bear the brand of Jesus Christ. We are the sheep of the LORD's pasture and He never leaves our side. The Shepherd is always concerned about the condition of His flock. Our very lives are in His hands.

God provides for all of our needs in His pasture. We graze on His Word. He leads us beside still waters to quench our thirst. He washes the dirt of sin off of us with the blood of Jesus. In His pasture, God protects us from our enemies and we are safe. He keeps track of each one of us and when we stray, He faithfully brings us back into the security of His pasture. As long as we stay in the pasture of our loving Shepherd we can fellowship with Him and with other believers. We are never alone. Do not stray away. Instead, worship the LORD with gladness for all He has done for you. Bless His holy name.

Manna Moment

Before you accepted Jesus Christ as your Savior, you went anywhere you wanted and did what you wanted. How has your life changed, since you have been walking with the LORD on the path He has put before you?

Day 123: Release of the Prisoners

"The LORD looked down from his sanctuary on high, from heaven he viewed the earth, to hear the groans of the prisoners and release those condemned to death."
—Psalm 102:19-20 (NIV)

Do you need to be released from imprisonment? What are the bars locking you in? Are you confined by fear and anxiety? Have the bars of loneliness and despair fenced you in? Does self-condemnation and guilt hold you as a prisoner? Call on the LORD and He will set you free. He hears the groaning and moaning of your heart. Cry out to Him in the hour of your deepest need. Jesus pardons the prisoners.

We were condemned to death but Jesus paid our debt and set us free. In Him, we have liberty and victory. We are free. Hallelujah!

Manna Moment

Take note of the invisible bars imprisoning you. Are bars of fear keeping you from being all God designed for you to be? Have you been singing the song that was written for your voice? Are you dancing the dance your feet were made for? Do you follow the dreams God places in your heart? Think about it and specifically ask the LORD to help you walk in the freedom He has provided.

Day 124: All His Benefits

Praise the LORD, O my soul; all my inmost being, praise his holy name. Praise the LORD, O my soul, and forget not all His benefits-who forgives all your sins and heals all your diseases, who redeems your life from the pit and crowns you with love and compassion, who satisfies your desires with good things so that your youth is renewed like the eagle's.
—Psalm 103:1-5 (NIV)

Thank God for all His benefits. He forgives and forgets all of our sins and heals our diseases. He redeems our life from death and hell. The LORD provides our needs and protects us from our enemies. May we never forget all the good things the LORD has done, is doing and will do in our lives. He crowns us with His love and compassion. Imagine, Almighty God, Creator of the universe, putting a beautiful crown on your head. This crown is made of His love and compassion and it will not perish, but last forever. He also satisfies our desires with good things so our youth is renewed and we can rise up and soar like eagles. Amen and hallelujah!

Manna Moment

Record all of God's wonderful benefits that are a part of your life. Give praise to the LORD.

Day 125: Saved, Healed and Rescued

"Then they cried to the LORD in their trouble, and he saved them from their distress. He sent forth his word and healed them; he rescued them from the grave."
—Psalm 107:19-20 (NIV)

The ear of Almighty God is always attentive to hear our cry. Like a loving mother with her newborn baby, the LORD is very concerned when He hears one of His children cry. When we are in trouble He saves us from our distress. He sends forth His Word, which gives us life and hope and heals us, physically and emotionally. His word heals our weary souls and wounded spirits. The LORD rescues us. He is our hero. Praise His holy name.

Manna Moment

Is anything troubling you? Are you distressed? Cry out to the LORD.

Day 126: Happiness, Success and Wealth

Happy are those who fear the LORD. Yes, happy are those who delight in doing what he commands. Their children will be successful everywhere; an entire generation of godly people will be blessed. They themselves will be wealthy, and their good deeds will never be forgotten.

—Psalm 112:1-3 (NLT)

Happiness, success and wealth are the goals of many people. Those who are not wise do many unscrupulous things to reach these goals. They betray co-workers, ruin their marriages, sacrifice their families and sell their souls to climb the ladder of success and wealth. The realization often comes too late that they have destroyed everyone in their life and are now unable to obtain the happiness they so desired. They may gain the material possessions but have no one left to share their lives with.

On the other hand God gives us an easier and more positive prescription for happiness and wealth as well as success for our children. His prescription is to fear the LORD and delight in doing His will. This Scripture is a beautiful promise. God is so good!

Manna Moment

No matter what we attain in this world, we are accountable to God to be responsible with the resources He has given us. Ask God to make you a wise and faithful steward of all you have been given.

Day 127: Call on the Name

The cords of death entangled me, the anguish of the grave came upon me; I was overcome by trouble and sorrow. Then I called on the name of the LORD: "O LORD, save me!" The LORD is gracious and righteous; our God is full of compassion.

—Psalm 116:3-5 (NIV)

Call on the name of the LORD. He not only listens to our prayers, but He also answers them. Ask Him to show you His way and His will for your life. Isaiah tells us to call on Him now, while He is near (Isaiah 55:6). Call on Him for everything you need. He longs to hear your voice.

In times of sickness, seek Jehovah Rophe, God the healer. If you are in a battle, call Jehovah Nissi, the God who aids in battle. In turmoil, cry out for Jehovah Shalom, the LORD, my peace. Are you lost? Summon the LORD my shepherd, Jehovah Rohi. If you are lonely call on Jehovah Shammah, God who is there.

Manna Moment

Assess your need. Call on the name that is most fitting to your need.

Day 128: He Has Been Good

Be at rest once more, O my soul, for the LORD has been good to you. For you, O LORD, have delivered my soul from death, my eyes from tears, my feet from stumbling,

that I may walk before the LORD in the land
of the living.

—Psalm 116:7-9 (NIV)

Praise the LORD! He has been wonderful to us. Each day He gives us to live is a special gift from Him. The LORD saved our souls from death and the pit of Hell by giving us the amazing gift of eternal life. Follow Him and He will keep your feet from stumbling by making the path ahead of you smooth. He is there to catch you when you trip. When it is a mountain you must climb, He gives you the strength to reach the top. As we walk in the land of the living and stay close to Him, our souls will rest in the goodness of the LORD.

Manna Moment

How have you experienced the goodness of the LORD?

Day 129: Set Free

In my anguish I cried to the LORD, and he
answered by setting me free. The LORD is
with me; I will not be afraid. What can man
do to me?

—Psalm 118:5-6 (NIV)

In John 8:32 Jesus said you shall know the truth and the truth shall make you free. Jesus also said He is the way, the truth, and the life (John 14:6). As we grow in our knowledge of Jesus we experience the freedom He gives. Jesus liberates us from the constraints our enemy utilizes to imprison us. He set us free from sin and death. We have been released from bondages to anxiety, worry and fear. In Jesus, the shackles of anger and shame are broken. The chains of unforgiveness and jealousy are destroyed.

Jesus came to set the captives free. We are free indeed! We are no longer confined by the enemy. Jesus removed the bars, it is our choice to walk out of the prison doors and follow Him down the narrow path that leads to life. He leads us to wide open spaces, green pastures, mountaintops and beside quiet waters. He offers us a life of liberty and abundance. Amen.

Manna Moment

Are you enjoying the life of freedom Jesus Christ made possible? If you are imprisoned in any area of your life, seek Jesus, who is the truth and ask Him to set you free.

Day 130: Wonderful Things in Your Law

Open my eyes that I may see wonderful things in your law.
—Psalm 119:18 (NIV)

May we open our eyes and hearts to see wonderful things in the Word of God. The Holy Bible is a love letter in which the Creator of the universe tells us that nothing will ever separate us from His love. The Word of God verifies our adoption into His family, by which we cry out, "Abba, Father." His Word is a will that details all we inherit as children of the King. The Holy Bible is an instruction manual, which directs our steps and tells us how to achieve success.

The Bible tells the remarkable story of creation, how it all started in the beginning. The Word also reveals the secrets regarding future events such as the formation of a new heaven and a new earth. It does not carry the latest news like today's newspaper but it does carry the most important news of God's salvation, grace and mercy which is available to every person through Jesus Christ.

The Word of God is alive and active and holds the power to transform lives when its principles are heeded. Open your eyes to see wonderful things in His Word.

Manna Moment

Set a positive tone for your day by reading the good news contained in the Holy Bible before you listen to or watch the worldly news.

Day 131: Hope and Preservation

Remember your word to your servant, for you have given me hope. My comfort in my suffering is this: Your promise preserves my life.

—Psalm 119:49-50 (NIV)

God gives us hope, the expectation and anticipation of something we yearn to see fulfilled. We expect success in all our endeavors. We hope for better times and cheerful days. We look forward to a healthy and fruitful life. We share the hope of joining Him one day and being with Him for all eternity. We have the hope of being with loved ones who are already in heaven.

Hope is like a spring gushing within us that energizes us to pursue a full satisfying life. In all of your suffering, trials and tribulations on this earth, hope for the best possible outcome and take comfort in His promise to preserve your life.

Manna Moment

What are you hoping to see, be or do before you leave this earth? Keep your hope alive by thinking and talking about your dreams daily.

Day 132: Where Does My Help Come From?

I lift up my eyes to the hills—where does my help come from? My help comes from the LORD, the Maker of heaven and earth.
—Psalm 121:1-2 (NIV)

Our help comes from the LORD. Are you overwhelmed with all that life brings your way? Look to the LORD for assistance. When your heart is deeply troubled and you do not know which way to go, lift your eyes up to the hills and follow Him. Direct your attention to the LORD when confronted with challenges that seem impossible. The God of possibilities is our helper. In all situations, your help will come from the LORD, the Maker of heaven and earth. Nothing is too difficult for the LORD. Praise Him!

Manna Moment

The LORD does not expect you to complete the mission He gave you, on your own. Appeal to Him for help.

Day 133: You Know Me

O LORD, you have searched me and you know me. You know when I sit and when I rise; you perceive my thoughts from afar. You discern my going out and my lying down; you are familiar with all my ways. Before a word is on my tongue you know it completely, O LORD.

—Psalm 139:1-4 (NIV)

Have you ever felt like someone got the wrong impression of you? Have you ever been completely misunderstood?

No one else may know the real you, but rest assured that the LORD is intimately acquainted with you. No person has the ability to know you like the One who created you. He searches the hidden recesses of your heart. The LORD perceives when a thought is conceived in your mind. He knows what you are going to say before you utter a sound. God is fully aware of all your struggles. He knows the depths of your pains and the sting of your disappointments. In His great love and understanding, God comforts you and heals your heart.

Manna Moment

If you could hide one thing from your heavenly Father, what would it be? Discuss this item with Him, knowing that you will not surprise Him, and you will feel better.

Day 134: Days Written In His Book

My frame was not hidden from you when I was made in the secret place. When I was woven together in the depths of the earth, your eyes saw my unformed body. All the days ordained for me were written in your book before one of them came to be.
—Psalm 139:15-16 (NIV)

God had His eyes on you before you were even born. He saw your unformed body and put it together in the womb of your mother. Not only did He form our bodies, He gave structure to our lives as well. He wrote all of our days down before we entered this world and drew our first breath. Sometimes we are surprised and caught off guard by the things that come our way, but they are no surprise to God. He already knows what each day holds for you.

And guess what? If God has already written down the day trouble comes your way, He has already written down the day He will bring you through those trials and tribulations as well. Know in your heart, that God has gone before you and prepared a way for you to walk through whatever comes your way. Your part is to persevere and trust God, no matter what.

Manna Moment

What direction has the LORD given you for the day? Follow the course He planned for you and He will successfully navigate you through.

Day 135: In the Morning

Let the morning bring me word of your unfailing love, for I have put my trust in you. Show me the way I should go, for to you I lift up my soul.
—Psalm 143:8 (NIV)

The beginning of each new day is a fresh start. When we get up in the morning the perfect opportunity exists for us to choose to go a different way and pursue the things we have been putting off. As the new day emerges decide to put your trust in the LORD and receive the word of His unfailing love.

Every morning, present your soul to the LORD. Offer yourself up to Him as the morning sacrifice and you will be filled with His everlasting love. At the beginning of your day, surrender control of the members of your body to God and to His will. Allow Him to guide you along on the path He has chosen for you.

Manna Moment

If you can speak these words to the LORD truthfully, say: "Here I am LORD. I present myself to you as a living sacrifice. I give you free reign in my heart and mind. May Your will be done in my life today."

Day 136: Faithful and Loving

The LORD is faithful to all his promises and loving toward all he has made. The LORD upholds all those who fall and lifts up all who are bowed down. The eyes of all look to you, and you give them their food at the proper time. You open your hand and satisfy the desires of every living thing.
—Psalm 145:13-16 (NIV)

The LORD is faithful and loving to all He has made. If you have fallen down He will sustain you. If you are hunched over from carrying heavy burdens, He will straighten you out and lighten your load. He satisfies the desires of every living thing, including you. He will satisfy your desires with an open hand.

Manna Moment

Think back to a time when God proved His faithfulness and love to you. Thank God for His faithfulness and love.

Day 137: Trust in the LORD

Trust in the LORD with all your heart and lean not on your own understanding; in all your ways acknowledge him, and he will make your paths straight.
—Proverbs 3:5-6 (NIV)

When you trust in the LORD with all your heart, you lay your understanding aside. Even if you cannot make sense out of events that have happened, you ought to blindly trust the LORD and His wisdom. God's way is higher than your way and His thoughts higher than your thoughts (Isaiah 55:9).

Once you completely trust God and fully rely on Him you are able to wait patiently for Him to show you the way. Whatever circumstances you are dealing with today, put your trust and confidence in the LORD. Trust Him to steer you in the right direction. He charted your course and He will do what is best for you. God is on your side and He will help you reach your desired destination successfully.

Manna Moment

Recall the last time you took action in the manner you preferred instead of the way God directed. What was the outcome? Whenever you are tempted to pick your own path, turn around and go with God.

Day 138: Love Covers All Offenses

Hatred stirs up quarrels, but love covers all offenses.
>   —Proverbs 10:12 (NLT)

When someone has offended you or wronged you in any way, you have the power to cover it up with love, pure unconditional love. The kind of love God shows us. Instead of getting all fired up, choose love. It is the higher way. Hatred and bitterness release poison into your system. The other person is not affected by you having an attitude with them. However, it hinders you from growing and experiencing the abundant life Jesus came to give us. No matter what the offense is, the Word says love covers them all. Imagine that.

I believe God pours His love into us continually so that we always have enough to extend to others. Even if they do not deserve it, we have done nothing to deserve the love God gives us. He just gives it to us because He is love. That is His nature. May we be like Him and love others, even if they have offended us.

Manna Moment

Have you been offended recently? Think about the person who offended you and think of some way you can show that person love. How does it make you feel to think of doing a kind act for someone who has wronged you? In spite of how you feel, take the action you need to take to cover the offense with love.

Day 139: Commit to the LORD

Commit to the LORD whatever you do, and your plans will succeed.
> —Proverbs 16:3 (NIV)

When we start a project or begin to execute a plan, our expectation and goal is to have it be successful. We do not begin endeavors wanting them to fail. The best guarantee to ensure success is to commit whatever you are about to do to the LORD. That means put it into the LORD's charge from beginning to end.

We do not want to forge ahead with our own ideas without consulting the LORD and then when things go awry start seeking Him. When we get an idea or start to put together a plan that is the time to submit it to the LORD. Ask Him for direction and guidance as you plan and begin to take action.

Manna Moment

When you start your day and make your plans. Consult with the LORD. If you are planning any new projects ask God to give you wisdom and direction.

Day 140: A Strong Tower

The name of the LORD is a strong tower; the righteous run to it and are safe.
—Proverbs 18:10 (NIV)

A strong tower is a safe place when the storms of life hit. A strong tower protects us in times of danger. A strong tower shelters us from the elements of life. It is a dwelling place. A strong tower offers shade from the scorching sun. It is a place of refuge and rest. This is what we have in the name of the LORD. If we run to the name of the LORD we will be safe.

Manna Moment

When trouble comes, do you run to the strong tower? When disaster knocks on your front door, take refuge in the namc of the LORD and be safe.

Day 141: Power of Life and Death

The tongue has the power of life and death, and those who love it will eat its fruit.
—Proverbs 18:21 (NIV)

We have the power to choose which words we will speak and which ones we will not speak. Everyday, we choose to speak words that bring life or death. Why choose death when you can choose life and experience a more abundant, fulfilling life? Instead of saying: "I can't," why not say "I can do all things through Christ." Instead of saying something is hard or difficult; say that it is easy and trouble-free. Instead of speaking about the lack in your present circumstances, talk about receiving the bountiful life that Jesus came to give us.

There is power in our words and we are to choose the words we speak carefully. Those who love life speak the words of life and enjoy the fruit of an extraordinary life. I encourage you today to choose words of life.

Manna Moment

Challenge yourself. See if you can go one day speaking only positive words and words of life. Then try to go thirty days.

Day 142: Receive Mercy

People who cover over their sins will not prosper. But if they confess and forsake them, they will receive mercy.
—Proverbs 28:13 (NLT)

It is impossible to hide our sins from God. We live a life open to His eyes, so we may as well admit our shortcomings to Him. He knows when we have missed the mark and He wants us to admit it so He can help us get back on the right track. If we confess our sins, He is faithful to forgive us of our sins. When we confess our sins, the blood of Jesus washes them away. When He died on the cross He paid the price for all sins, past sins, present sins and future sins. Once we confess our sins we must give them up and let them go. It is when we confess them and turn away from them that we receive God's mercy. Mercy is the compassion or kindness God shows to us, even though we do not deserve it. May you receive His mercy today.

Manna Moment

Think of all the ways you have received God's mercy. Search your heart to see if there are any sins you are attempting to justify or make excuses for. Confess them and receive mercy.

143: Reach Out and Help

Two are better than one, because they have a good return for their work: If one falls down, his friend can help him up. But pity the man who falls and has no one to help him up!
—Ecclesiastes 4:9-10 (NIV)

There is nothing like having a true friend to help you in times of need. What a consolation to have someone there for you, with listening ears, when you need to talk to someone. It elevates the spirit to have someone encourage you when you are feeling down. Friendship is a special gift from God. Be a genuine friend to the people God has placed in your life.

Manna Moment

Think of a person you can reach out to. Help lift that person up with the love of Jesus.

144: Under a Cloud

And this, too, is a very serious problem. As people come into this world, so they depart. All their hard work is for nothing. They have been working for the wind, and everything will be swept away. Throughout their lives, they live under a cloud – frustrated, discouraged, and angry.

—Ecclesiastes 5:16-17 (NLT)

Do you know someone who seems to be living their life under a cloud of gloom and doom? How many times have you felt your life was under a dark cloud? No matter what you did or which way you turned, you were unable to see the light. How often are you frustrated because it seems like nothing ever goes your way? Perhaps, you are discouraged because you think nothing will ever work out the way you desire. Do you get angry because it seems like others have great lives and work very little or not at all? Maybe you are angry because you worked hard for a promotion and it was given to someone who did not deserve it or was not even qualified.

At times like these, it does us good to remember that God is still on the throne and He is working for our good. We should not look at our present circumstances and lose all hope for better days. Our current situation is no reflection of our future triumph and glory. We serve a faithful God of hope and victory. Come out from under the cloud and step into the sunshine.

Manna Moment

Are you frustrated, discouraged or angry? Leave the dark, cloudy skies behind and live your life in the light of the LORD and your path will shine brighter and brighter. As you walk in the light with the LORD, any frustration, discouragement and anger will melt away.

Day 145: A Gift of God

Moreover, when God gives any man wealth and possessions, and enables him to enjoy them, to accept his lot and be happy in his work – this is a gift of God. He seldom reflects on the days of his life, because God keeps him occupied with gladness of heart.
—Ecclesiastes 5:19-20 (NIV)

We are to be like the Apostle Paul and learn to be content in whatever circumstances come our way.

Being content does not mean we cease striving to improve our situation and expand our territory. It means we recognize we are where God wants us and it is not a permanent position. We are on a journey, constantly moving, always growing and becoming all God wants us to be.

The word tells us that God, who began a good work in us, will be faithful to complete it. The ability to live a life of contentment in all situations and to enjoy the work of our hands is a gift of God. When we achieve this state of mind, our past sorrows will fade into the background of our lives and the focal point will be the gladness that fills our heart.

Manna Moment

Are you happy in your current line of work? Continue to perform your duties with an attitude of excellence and with the knowledge that you are working for God. Do all that is in your power to position yourself for the next move. That may mean getting more training or education or just honing in on your skills. Be content and patient as you continue to pray until God opens the door for advancement or change.

Day 146: No Flaw

"All beautiful you are, my darling; there is no flaw in you."

—Song of Songs 4:7 (NIV)

Here we have a picture of love between a man and a woman. He loves her so much, he can see no flaw in her. Reminds me of the Scripture in 1 Peter 4:8 which says love covers a multitude of sins. Then I ask myself, "Do I walk in a love with others so real, that it covers their sins and I do not see any flaws in them?" Not! This is truly an aspiration for us all, to love one another so deeply we cannot see the other person's flaws. That would blow our enemy away.

What does this kind of love look like? It looks like the kind of love Jesus displayed when He died on the cross to save us: self-sacrificing. It looks like the love God shows to us everyday, a forgiving love, an unconditional love, and a love that sees people for what they can become. I challenge you to love until you can no longer see the flaw in the other person.

Manna Moment

Is there someone you have difficulty walking in love with? Make it a point to show this person unconditional love. Accept them the way they are and look at the good in them.

Day 147: Fear the LORD Only

Do not be afraid that some plan conceived behind closed doors will be the end of you. Do not fear anything except the LORD Almighty. He alone is the Holy One. If you fear him, you need fear nothing else.
　　　　　　　　　　—Isaiah 8:12-13 (NLT)

175

We have all been the target of some plan that was conceived behind closed doors. When others lie to you, betray you, or plot and scheme against you, have no fear because we serve a mighty God and He has power, dominion and authority over all. The LORD can handle any darts the enemy throws your way. The only person we need fear is the LORD God Almighty and Him alone.

Manna Moment

Are you fearful of what others may do to you or what they may say about you? How does this fear impede your mission for the LORD? Seek deliverance from the LORD and meditate on Psalm 27:1-2 and Psalm 34:4.

Day 148: Perfect Faithfulness

O LORD, you are my God; I will exalt you and praise your name, for in perfect faithfulness you have done marvelous things, things planned long ago.
You have been a refuge for the poor, a refuge for the needy in his distress, a shelter from the storm and a shade from the heat.
—Isaiah 25:1, 4 (NIV)

Praise the Lord for His perfect faithfulness! He is always faithful. His faithfulness is flawless and it never ends. You can count on Him to be all that you need: a strong rock to stand on, a refuge of safety to hide in, a shelter of protection, a cooling shade, a sturdy shield, a fortress to retreat in, a dwelling place to reside in, and a strong foundation for support. Hallelujah!

Manna Moment

How has God's perfect faithfulness been displayed in your life?

Day 149: Perfect Peace

You will keep in perfect peace all who trust in you, whose thoughts are fixed on you! Trust in the LORD always, for the LORD GOD is the eternal Rock.
                                        —Isaiah 26:3-4 (NLT)

Keep your thoughts fixed on the LORD and you will have perfect peace. His peace will reign in your mind, in your spirit and in your soul. You will feel it deep down in your heart. The peace of God soothes frayed nerves and calms emotions that are set on edge. He is the eternal Rock, the One you can stand on and know that He will always be there for you.

Manna Moment

When you feel anxiety mounting say to yourself, "The LORD keeps those who trust in Him in perfect peace. I trust in you LORD and I receive Your perfect peace now."

Day 150: In Quietness and Confidence

The Sovereign LORD, the Holy One of Israel, says, "Only in returning to me and waiting for me will you be saved. In quietness and confidence is your strength."
—Isaiah 30:15 (NLT)

We find strength as we quietly and patiently wait for the LORD, with no complaining or murmuring. We gain strength, emotionally, spiritually and physically, when we put our confidence in the LORD and His ability to handle everything that concerns us. May you wait on the Lord and gain new strength.

Manna Moment

Are you feeling weak? Renew your strength by putting all your confidence in the LORD and sitting quietly in His presence.

Day 151: He Is Waiting for You

But the LORD still waits for you to come to him so he can show you his love and compassion. For the LORD is a faithful God. Blessed are those who wait for him to help them.
—Isaiah 30:18 (NLT)

Have you gazed into the eyes of the LORD today? He is waiting for you to come to Him. Jesus tells us to come, just the way we are. The fact that we come to Him is much more important than the condition in which we come. It does not matter whether you are angry, bitter, depressed, fearful, beat up, down and out or upbeat, loving, forgiving and full of joy. He wants to see you. He desires to express His unfailing love and everlasting compassion. After you go to Him, wait patiently for His help and you will be blessed.

Manna Moment

Do you want to keep the LORD of the universe waiting? Run to Him without delay, wait for His help and receive all the blessings He has for you.

Day 152: Close to His Heart

He tends his flock like a shepherd: He gathers the lambs in his arms and carries them close to his heart; he gently leads those that have young.
—Isaiah 40:11 (NIV)

The Sovereign LORD takes care of His people like a shepherd tends to his flock. He gathers us up in His arms and carries us close to His heart because He loves us. We matter to God. We are important to Him. He knows our pain and our struggles. In His arms, He shelters us from the storms of life. In His arms, the strength of the LORD becomes our strength. When we are in His arms we can rest and be at peace.

Manna Moment

Close your eyes and visualize being carried close to the heart of our loving Savior. Close enough to hear the beat of His heart. Close enough to smell the sweet fragrance of His love and compassion. Feel the warmth of His arms as they wrap around you. Enjoy this special place you occupy, close to the heart of the Shepherd.

Day 153: Wait on the LORD

But those who wait on the LORD will find new strength. They will fly high on wings like eagles. They will run and not grow weary. They will walk and not faint.
—Isaiah 40:31 (NLT)

Instead of frantically rushing around attempting to live life by our own strength, the Word instructs us to wait on the LORD. When issues arise in our lives, we are not to immediately try to deal with the situation the way we *think* it needs to be handled. Rather, we should spend some time with God. Go to Him and ask Him how the situation should be handled. Seek His direction, wisdom and guidance. Allow Him to lead you in His perfect timing.

As we wait on the LORD we find new strength. This new strength from the LORD gives us the ability to run and not grow weary. When we wait on the LORD we will walk and not grow faint. We will fly high on the wings of His Spirit and He will be the wind beneath our wings. Yes, wait on the LORD.

Manna Moment

Are you searching for a solution to an ongoing problem that is wearing you out? Seek divine guidance for the situations you face and then wait on the LORD for direction and renewed strength.

Day 154: Help Is Here

So do not fear, for I am with you; do not be dismayed, for I am your God. I will strengthen you and help you; I will uphold you with my righteous right hand.

For I am the LORD, your God, who takes hold of your right hand and says to you, Do not fear; I will help you.

—Isaiah 41:10, 13 (NIV)

Do not fear because the LORD is with you. There is no reason to be distraught. You are not without help. And look who you have to help: the LORD, our Creator and our Redeemer. He runs to our aid in times of trouble. He knows exactly what we need and when we need it. He supports us with His victorious right hand. Nothing or no one can stand against the LORD. With our hand in His, we are more than conquerors.

Manna Moment

Who do you turn to for help in times of trouble? Reach out to God and tell Him what you need.

Day 155: I Will Be With You

When you pass through the waters, I will be with you; and when you pass through the rivers, they will not sweep over you. When you walk through the fire, you will not be burned; the flames will not set you ablaze. For I am the LORD, your God, the Holy One of Israel, your Savior;
—Isaiah 43:2-3 (NIV)

Throughout the course of our lives, we go through various phases. At times we go through the rivers and then there are times when fiery trials blaze. Sometimes it seems like you are going to drown in the waters of adversity. You try desperately to come up for air but the seaweeds of life are tangled around your ankles and they pull you down.

Sometimes, the path you are on leads you through the fire. You can feel the intense heat surrounding you. You hear the rumble of the blaze as it devours whatever it touches, and refuses to be quenched. You keep walking as the raging flames threaten to engulf you. In both of these situations, keep moving forward. The LORD says you will not drown and you will not be burned. He will be with you and He will see you through. Praise the LORD!

Manna Moment

If you are passing through the rivers or walking through the fire, recall how the LORD made you aware of His presence in your last trial. Praise the LORD for His faithfulness.

Day 156: He Is Making a Way

"Forget the former things; do not dwell on the past. See, I am doing a new thing! Now it springs up; do you not perceive it? I am making a way in the desert and streams in the wasteland."
— Isaiah 43:18-19 (NIV)

God is doing a new thing. We must let go of anything we are holding onto from the past. Let go of all past offenses, resentments, disappointments and hurts. It is hard to move forward when we are still looking back at where we have been. Remember Lot's wife. She was turned into a pillar of salt because she looked back after being warned by the angel, "Don't look back." Praise the Lord for the new things He is doing in your life. He is making a way for you. He is making your path smooth and straight.

Manna Moment

Are you dwelling on something from the past? Let go of the past and look at the new thing the LORD is doing in your life.

Day 157: Peace and Righteousness

If only you had paid attention to my commands,
your peace would have been like a river, your
righteousness like the waves of the sea.
　　　　　　　　　　—Isaiah 48:18 (NIV)

When we follow the LORD's commands our peace flows and we have a constant stream of righteousness. We are at peace with God and with our own conscience. As we follow His commands our righteousness consistently rolls in one wave after another. When we fall short, we have Jesus Christ as our righteousness. Praise the Lord!

Manna Moment

Recall a time you did not follow the LORD's commands. Were the results disastrous? Was your soul in a state of turmoil and your conscience stained with guilt? Seek to obey His command and maintain your peace and righteousness.

Day 158: We Will Triumph

Because the Sovereign LORD helps me, I will
not be dismayed. Therefore, I have set my
face like a stone, determined to do his will.
And I know that I will triumph.
　　　　　　　　　　—Isaiah 50:7 (NLT)

When we do the LORD's will, we have His help and we can be certain we will be triumphant. Those who trust in the LORD will be victorious over all. As we yield to His will we shall overcome whatever life brings our way. Do not crumble under the winds of adversity. Do not cave in to the mounting pressures of life. Set your face like a stone, commit to do His will and enjoy the sweet taste of victory.

Manna Moment

In what situations has pure determination to do His will brought about triumph? Think about past victories during times of battle.

Day 159: A Man of Sorrows

He was despised and rejected by men, a man of sorrows, and familiar with suffering. Like one from whom men hid their faces he was despised, and we esteemed him not. Surely he took our infirmities and carried our sorrows, yet we considered him stricken by God, smitten by him, and afflicted. But he was pierced for our transgressions, he was crushed for our iniquities; the punishment that brought us peace was upon him, and by his wounds we are healed.
—Isaiah 53:3-5 (NIV)

Our Lord and Savior, Jesus Christ, is well acquainted with sorrows and suffering. He carried our sorrows and was pierced for our transgressions. He was crushed for our iniquities. He knows what it means to be despised and rejected. He accepted the punishment for our sins and brought us peace with God. By His wounds we are made whole. Praise the Lord! In all of our trials and tribulations may we think of the Lord Jesus Christ, who paid the highest price of all with His life.

Manna Moment

Take a few minutes to reflect on all that Jesus Christ suffered to save us. Thank the Lord for His sacrifice.

Day 160: Be Revived

For this is what the high and lofty One says— he who lives forever, whose name is holy: "I live in a high and holy place, but also with him who is contrite and lowly in spirit, to revive the spirit of the lowly and to revive the heart of the contrite."

—Isaiah 57:15 (NIV)

God dwells with those who repent of their sins and offenses and have a humble spirit. God dwells in a high place, but He also dwells with you and with me. No matter how far down our emotions and life situations may drag us, God is there with us.

God says He lives with us to revive our spirits and our hearts. He wants to bring us back to life and make our spirit fresh and strong. He wants us to be useful for His kingdom. This is revival. Allow your spirit and your heart to be revived by Almighty God, today.

Manna Moment

Do something to revive your physical body today. Take a relaxing bath. Visit a day spa. Take a nap. Appreciate one of the natural wonders of God by watching the sun rise or set, sit on the beach and watch the waves come rolling in, hike up a mountain or drive along a country road and take in the scenery.

Day 161: He Acts on Your Behalf

Since ancient times no one has heard, no ear has perceived, no eye has seen any God besides you, who acts on behalf of those who wait for him.
—Isaiah 64:4 (NIV)

Our God is faithful. If you wait for Him, you can be confident that He will act on your behalf. He strengthens you in weakness. He brings healing to your sick body. When you are falsely accused, He brings the truth to light. If your heart is broken and shattered, God will make it whole. He clears up doubt and confusion and gives faith and direction. If you are imprisoned, He sets you free. Wait patiently for God and He will act on your behalf.

Manna Moment

Are you waiting for God to act on your behalf? As you wait, review past ordeals God carried you through. If you know someone who has gone through similar situations ask them to share their testimony with you.

Day 162: We Are the Clay

Yet, O LORD, you are our Father. We are the clay, you are the potter; we are all the work of your hand.
—Isaiah 64:8 (NIV)

We are the clay in the hands of our heavenly Father. He is the potter who molds us and shapes us according to His will and purpose. We are to be soft and pliable like clay in His hands. We are to be flexible. When it is time to take on a different shape let us give way to the design of the Potter. May we always be responsive to the touch of the Master' hands, as He makes us into a vessel that is fit for His use, a perfect masterpiece with His unique signature.

Manna Moment

Play with some play dough or clay. Notice how it conforms to the shape you give it. When you press it or roll it, you get no resistance. It does not rise up in rebellion. That is how we are to be in the hands of our heavenly Father.

Day 163: Like a Tree by the Water

But blessed is the man who trusts in the LORD, whose confidence is in him. He will be like a tree planted by the water that sends out its roots by the stream. It does not fear when heat comes; its leaves are always green. It has no worries in a year of drought and never fails to bear fruit.
—Jeremiah 17:7-8 (NIV)

When we completely trust in the LORD we are like a tree planted near water. Once we place all of our confidence in the LORD, our roots grow deep, connecting us to Jesus, the living water. Jesus provides all we need to mature and bear fruit, as our roots draw from Him. With the LORD as our source we bear the fruit of joy, peace, patience, love and kindness. Then we can share them with those God places in our lives.

Nurtured by the living water, we grow strong and are able to withstand cold, windy storms. During the hot, dry season we do not faint or grow weary. We are not consumed with fear of drought, because we know we have an everlasting supply of fresh, cool, *living water*. Like a tree planted by the water, we stand tall and firm. We are firm in our faith and secure in our relationship with Jesus.

Manna Moment

In what ways can your roots grow deeper in the LORD? Follow the steps you identified so you can flourish in the garden of the LORD.

Day 164: Plans for You

"For I know the plans I have for you," declares the LORD, "plans to prosper you and not to harm you, plans to give you hope and a future."

—Jeremiah 29:11 (NIV)

Nothing that happens to us is a surprise to God. He has a master plan for our lives. Plans that are designed to make us welcome each new day with great expectation of what God is going to accomplish in our lives that day. Eagerly watch God's plan unfold in your life today and everyday!

Manna Moment

What plans do you have for the rest of your life? Ask God to reveal the plans He has for you.

Day 165: Seek and Find

Then you will call upon me and come and pray to me, and I will listen to you. You will

*seek me and find me when you seek me with
all your heart.*
—Jeremiah 29:12-13 (NIV)

This scripture is part of a letter the prophet
Jeremiah sent from Jerusalem to the Israelites while
they were exiled to Babylon. Even though they had
forsaken the LORD, He still reached out to them
and instructed them on how to find their way back
to Him.

If you have strayed away from the heavenly
Father, these words still apply. When you call upon
the LORD and pray to Him, He is listening. His ear
is always receptive to your call. When you seek the
LORD with all of your heart, you will find Him.

Manna Moment

Has the path you are traveling on taken you away
from the LORD? Invest your time and energy into
seeking the LORD wholeheartedly and you will find
Him.

Day 166: He Heals Your Wounds

*"But I will restore you to health and heal
your wounds," declares the LORD...*
—Jeremiah 30:17 (NIV)

The LORD heals our physical, emotional and
spiritual wounds. The wounds may be physical,
as a result of an accident or war injury. If we were

betrayed by people we trust we have experienced emotional wounds. We may have suffered emotional trauma by harsh words that were spoken to us. At times we are spiritually wounded because it seems as though God let us down due to some tragedy we experienced.

God heals our wounds and restores us to a state of good health. When His restoration project is complete our body functions normally, we feel good, uplifted and full of joy and our thoughts are positive. Once we are spiritually restored we are full of faith and lean totally on the LORD, who makes us whole.

Manna Moment

What lesions do you have festering? Turn your wounded areas over to the curative power of God in prayer.

Day 167: Be Refreshed!

This is what the LORD Almighty, the God of Israel says: . . . "I will refresh the weary and satisfy the faint."
—Jeremiah 31:23, 25 (NIV)

Are you weary from the journey life has you on right now? Are you feeling faint hearted, like you just do not have the strength to go on? Do the demands of each day leave you feeling crushed and lifeless?

If you are weary, worn out and about to fall apart, call on the LORD. Sit at the feet of our Lord and

Savior, Jesus Christ and be refreshed and renewed, physically and spiritually. Take time out of your busy schedule to lay your head in His lap and let Him gently pat you on the head. Make the divine connection. He is the vine and we are the branches (John 15:5). May we hook up to our living Source and draw from Him all that we need.

Manna Moment

Think of how good it feels when you take a break and let the LORD refresh you. How often do you desire to be refreshed? The LORD is there waiting for you.

Day 168: Nothing Too Hard

"Ah, Sovereign LORD, you have made the heavens and the earth by your great power and outstretched arm. Nothing is too hard for you."
—Jeremiah 32:17 (NIV)

The situations confronting you are never too hard for God to handle. There is no set of circumstances that baffles God. All wisdom and knowledge belong to Him. In His great power, He made the heavens and the earth. Could any problem or challenge we have be any more difficult or complicated?

Manna Moment

What difficult situation are you facing right now? Give it to God in prayer.

Day 169: In the Mud

So they took Jeremiah and put him into the cistern of Malkijah, the king's son, which was in the courtyard of the guard. They lowered Jeremiah by ropes into the cistern; it had no water in it, only mud, and Jeremiah sank down into the mud.
—Jeremiah 38:6 (NIV)

Jeremiah, the prophet, was unjustly thrown into a cistern by the officials of King Zedekiah, for speaking the word of the LORD. Can you relate to Jeremiah? Have you been let down? Do walls of darkness surround you? Are you sinking into the mud?

Here are two things to remember. First, you are not alone. God is with you in the deep dark well. He never leaves you. Secondly, even though you are immersed in mud, God will not allow it to bury you. Jeremiah was pulled up out of the cistern with ropes. Likewise, God will lift you up again!

Manna Moment

Are you emotionally down in the bottom of a muddy cistern? Hold onto the rope of the LORD and He will pull you up.

Day 170: New Every Morning

Because of the LORD's great love we are not consumed, for his compassions never fail. They are new every morning; great is your faithfulness. I say to myself, "The LORD is my portion; therefore I will wait for him."
                    —Lamentations 3:22-24 (NIV)

The LORD's compassion for us starts over with the dawn of each new day. We cannot wear it out and it never grows stale. God designed life to be taken one day at a time. He grouped our days together in twenty-four hour increments because He knew how much we could endure before we needed rest, sleep and a clean start. Thank God for brand new compassions emerging every morning. With the commencement of each day we receive a fresh outpouring of His compassion.

Manna Moment

How can you impart compassion to the people God brings your way today? Remember you can be generous with His compassion, knowing that you will be given a fresh filling every morning.

Day 171: Wait Quietly

The LORD is good to those whose hope is in him, to the one who seeks him; it is good to wait quietly for the salvation of the LORD.
                    —Lamentations 3:25-26 (NIV)

First, seek the LORD. Then, wait in silence for the LORD until you sense His calm presence and hear His still small voice. Wait quietly to receive His gentle touch and comforting hug. Let your soul rest while you receive word of His unfailing love. Allow His Holy Spirit to fill you with power from on High. Wait quietly for His grace and salvation to come to you and your loved ones.

Manna Moment

Seek God in a time of prayer or praise and then wait quietly for Him to respond.

Day 172: Lost, Injured or Weak?

"I will search for the lost and bring back the strays. I will bind up the injured and strengthen the weak . . ."
—Ezekiel 34:16 (NIV)

Do you have a son or a daughter, a brother or a sister who has strayed off the narrow path that leads to eternal life? Has Mom or Dad lost their way? God seeks out your lost loved ones. He has not forgotten them.

Are you lost? When you are deceived and fleshly desires cause you to stray, God will bring you back. For those who are suffering injury or brokenness, God will bind up your wounds. His tender touch heals you. In times of weakness, God gives you strength. Praise the LORD for His goodness to us!

Manna Moment

Who would you like to put on the list for the
LORD to find? Intercede to the LORD on their
behalf.

Day 173: Look Carefully and Listen Closely

*I looked and saw the glory of the LORD filling
the temple of the LORD, and I fell facedown.
The LORD said to me, "Son of man, look
carefully, listen closely and give attention to
everything I tell you concerning all the regu-
lations regarding the temple of the LORD."*
—Ezekiel 44:4-5 (NIV)

In the above Scripture, the LORD is speaking
to Ezekiel about giving attention to His instructions
concerning the temple of the LORD. However, we
are to look carefully and listen closely whenever the
LORD gives us any kind of direction.

What might you hear when you look carefully for
the LORD? If we give our full attention to the environment around us, we notice the glory of the LORD.
His mighty works declare His glory. The rising and
setting of the sun has the signature of God on it. The
splendor of the moon and the twinkling of the stars in
the sky bear His brilliance.

What might you hear when you listen closely for
the voice of the LORD? Will you hear His voice in a
boom of thunder or will a gentle wind carry the sound

of His voice to your ears? You may hear Him speak to you through the pages of His Word. If you listen closely you will hear His still small voice whispering about how much He loves you. Be careful to obey every instruction of the LORD. He knows what is best for each one of us.

Manna Moment

Fall facedown before the LORD. Listen closely for the words He speaks to your heart. As you go through your day, look carefully to see His glory all around you.

Day 174: God Gives Wisdom and Knowledge

"Praise be to the name of God for ever and ever; wisdom and power are his. He changes times and seasons; he sets up kings and deposes them. He gives wisdom to the wise and knowledge to the discerning. He reveals deep and hidden things; he knows what lies in darkness, and light dwells with him."
—Daniel 2:20-22 (NIV)

All wisdom and authority belong to our God. He gives wisdom and knowledge to those who search for it. He commands the times and the seasons. God has an appointed time and season for all things. As the times and seasons of our lives change may we seek His insight to gain understanding. He reveals the deep and hidden things to those with eyes to see. Even the darkness is not dark to Him. Be enlightened by the Holy Spirit and make your home in the light with God.

Manna Moment

Ask God for wisdom and knowledge that will equip you to live each day in line with His perfect will. Profess Proverbs 2:10 which says, wisdom will enter your heart and knowledge will be pleasant to your soul.

Day 175: Fiery Furnace

And these three men, Shadrach, Meshach, and Abed-Nego, fell down bound into the midst of the burning fiery furnace. Then King Nebuchadnezzar was astonished; and he rose in haste and spoke, saying to his counselors, "Did we not cast three men bound into the midst of the fire?" They answered and said to the king, "True, O king." "Look!" he answered, "I see four men loose, walking in the midst of the fire; and they are not hurt, and the form of the fourth is like the Son of God."
—Daniel 3:23-25 (NKJ)

At times, it seems like we are in the midst of a fiery furnace. But praise God, His word is true and He is faithful. Here are some reminders for our fiery trials. Even though we feel the enemy has us bound,

Jesus Christ has set us free and He continues to set us free everyday from whatever thoughts, feelings, lies or circumstances come our way. We may feel we are in the fiery furnace alone, but we need to remember, we are not alone. The Son of God is with us wherever we go, even in the fiery furnace. Even though we are in a blazing furnace we are free to keep moving, keep walking right on through. We do not have to stop and become paralyzed. There is nothing to be gained by pausing to have a pity party. Make sure you do not fall down. Instead, keep walking on the Word of God all the way through the fiery furnace.

Even though the sweltering furnace may be heated seven times more than it usually is, always remember, like Shadrach, Meshach and Abednego, "…our God whom we serve is able to deliver us from the burning fiery furnace, and He will deliver us…" (Daniel 3:17 NKJ). When all is said and done, the smell of fire does not even have to be on us.

Manna Moment

Think of a time when you felt the flames of a fiery furnace. What lessons have you learned in the fiery furnace experiences of your life?

Day 176: He Rescues and He Saves

"I issue a decree that in every part of my kingdom people must fear and reverence the God of Daniel. For he is the living God and he endures forever; his kingdom will not be

destroyed, his dominion will never end. He rescues and he saves; he performs signs and wonders in the heavens and on the earth. He rescued Daniel from the power of the lions."
—Daniel 6:26-27 (NIV)

First Peter 5:8 tells us our enemy, the devil prowls around like a roaring lion looking for someone to devour. If you are feeling trapped in the lion's den today, know in your heart that our God rescues and He saves. God will not allow the lion to consume you. I pray that He would perform signs and wonders in your life today.

Manna Moment

Are you crouched in the lion's den overwhelmed by fear and anxiety? Continue to serve God faithfully and He will rescue you and save you from the den of your enemies.

Day 177: Deeply Loved

"Don't be afraid," he said, "for you are deeply loved by God. Be at peace; take heart and be strong!"
—Daniel 10:19 (NLT)

You are deeply loved by God. May all of God's people really understand how wide, how long, how high and how deep is the love of God. When we hold onto the love God has for us, our souls will abide in peace and His love will give us strength. When we truly understand the depth of God's love for us, everything else fades into the background of our lives. Nothing on this earth compares with His glorious, unfailing, unending, unconditional love. No person is capable of loving us as deeply and completely as our Heavenly Father. Praise His name!

Manna Moment

How often do you think about the immense love God has for you? When is your heart most deeply touched by the love of God? Seek out a deeper understanding of God's multifaceted love.

Day 178: Knowledge Needed

My people are destroyed from lack of knowledge.
—Hosea 4:6 (NIV)

The prophet Hosea spoke these words to the Israelites at a time when they had deserted the LORD and even refused to acknowledge Him. When we reject the knowledge of the LORD the results are disastrous. We are destroyed spiritually and sometimes even physically.

James, the apostle and brother of Jesus, says if we lack wisdom, we should ask God. In James 4:2, he goes on to say we do not have, because we do not ask. Instead of wandering aimlessly through life, under a dark cloud of ignorance and confusion, ask

God for the wisdom and knowledge to successfully get you through the circumstances of your life. Seek God and the wisdom He freely gives.

Manna Moment

What knowledge do you need to effectively resolve the dilemmas before you? Ask God for the wisdom to apply that knowledge appropriately.

Day 179: Press On to Know Him

"Oh, that we might know the LORD! Let us press on to know him! Then he will respond to us as surely as the arrival of dawn or the coming of rains in early spring."
—Hosea 6:3 (NLT)

With so many distractions in the world, it takes a very deliberate act of our will and a strong desire in our hearts to press on to know the LORD. From the moment we wake up to the buzz of the alarm clock we are bombarded with sounds and schedules and demands on our time. Telephones ring, televisions blare and radios boom. E-mails flow continuously in our inbox. Horns blow and brakes screech as we make our way through traffic. And our day continues on in this manner until we collapse in bed at the end of our day.

Be like Jesus and get alone and spend time with the heavenly Father. Enter into the Holy Place, the place where His Holy Spirit dwells, in the sanctuary of your heart. Be real and open your heart to Him. Tell Him what is on your mind. Be still. At some point, be quiet and listen to what He speaks to your heart.

If we pray Matthew 6:11, "Give us our food for today," we have to take the time to sit down and eat at the LORD's table and drink from the cup of His blessings. It is difficult to enjoy a meal while you are on the run. Press on to know Him. You will not be disappointed. He will respond.

Manna Moment

Let the world around you fade away for a few minutes, while you press on to know the Lord.

Day 180: Call On the Name and Be Saved

And everyone who calls on the name of the LORD will be saved.
                              —Joel 2:32 (NIV)

Call on the name of the LORD and you will receive salvation. Notice this verse says *everyone* and not *some* people who call on the name will be saved. Everyone includes you and me.

He not only redeems us from death and hell with the special gift of eternal life, the LORD also saves us from sickness because He is the One who heals us and makes us complete. The hope He gives lifts us out of depression. He delivers us from weariness by giving us a more bountiful life. He rescues us from darkness because He is the Light. He takes away our poverty by issuing heavenly riches to us. He saves us from our weaknesses because He is our strength. He saves us when we are lonely because He is always with us. He is our constant companion.

Manna Moment

What do you need to be saved from? Call on the wonderful name of the LORD!

Day 181: Seek Good

Seek good, not evil, that you may live. Then the LORD God Almighty will be with you, just as you say he is.
—Amos 5:14 (NIV)

Seek the good in every situation and you will live the abundant life Jesus came to give us. In Psalm 119:68, the psalmist tells us that the LORD is good, and what He does is good. If we strive to be like Him and act like Him (loving, compassionate and forgiving) our lives will be enriched, and our fruit will be good. Hearts will be softened, relationships restored and healing will take place. Furthermore, Almighty God will be with you wherever you go.

Manna Moment

Think of a situation that has gone awry. Ask God to reveal how you can turn it around by doing good.

Day 182: Pride and Deception

"The pride of your heart has deceived you, you who live in the clefts of the rocks and make your home on the heights, you who say to yourself, 'Who can bring me down to the ground?' Though you soar like the eagle and make your nest among the stars, from there I will bring you down," declares the LORD.

— Obadiah 3-4 (NIV)

The book of Obadiah is a prophecy of judgment against the nation of Edom for their prideful attitude and their abuse of the Israelites. The LORD's reaction to Edom's pride can serve as a warning for us to stay away from pride and deception because of the downward spiral that is sure to follow.

As we accomplish more of the things we desire and have worked hard for, there is a risk of forgetting God who made it possible. Once we reach our career goals—and live in the neighborhood of our choice, in the home of our dreams, driving the car we fantasized about, with our kids in our favorite Christian school—there is the danger of taking our eyes off of God and letting our egos inflate with pride. If we begin to think more highly of ourselves than we ought to, we are caught in the trap of self-deception and are headed for destruction.

During times of prosperity and success let us keep our eyes on God, who gave us the wisdom, the knowledge and the strength to acquire all we have. When we receive accolades from friends, co-workers and neighbors we should always give the glory to God. Stay clear of pride and deception by keeping your spirit humble and your heart appreciative for all God has done in your life.

Manna Moment

What successes have you recently celebrated? Did you thank God? Take a few minutes to praise God for all that He is doing in your life. Thank Him for all He has already done.

Day 183: Running Away from the Lord

The word of the LORD came to Jonah son of Amittai: "Go to the great city of Nineveh and preach against it, because its wickedness has come up before me." But Jonah ran away from the LORD and headed for Tarshish. He went down to Joppa, where he found a ship bound for that port. After paying the fare, he went aboard and sailed for Tarshish to flee from the LORD.

—Jonah 1:1-3 (NIV)

Have you ever felt like Jonah? Maybe you turned left when God said go right. Maybe He asked you to do something for someone and you didn't want to do it for that particular person or it was not a convenient time for you. Remember, He still loves you and forgives your transgressions when you confess them to Him. In spite of Jonah's disobedience, the LORD provided a great fish to swallow him up when he was thrown overboard. In Jonah's distress he called upon the LORD. And He rescued Jonah by causing the fish to vomit Jonah onto dry land.

When Jonah paid the fare to board that ship, he probably had no idea what his disobedience was going to cost him. Sometimes the price we pay for disobedience is more than we want to pay. The sin often keeps us longer than we want to stay and takes us further away from God than we intended. As we can see with Jonah, no matter where we are or how we arrived there God listens to our cry. And in His great and mighty compassion and love He answers us.

Manna Moment

Are you running away from the LORD and His will for you? Turn around and run toward God and He will receive you with open arms.

Day 184: God Brings Us Up from the Pit

I went down to the moorings of the mountains; The earth with its bars closed behind me forever; Yet You have brought up my life from the pit, O LORD, my God.

When my soul fainted within me, I remembered the LORD; And my prayer went up to You, into Your holy temple.

—Jonah 2:6-7 (NKJ)

Is your life in a pit? We have all been there. There are all kinds of emotional pits we find ourselves descending into. We may not want to go there but before we know it our emotions plunge down until we hit rock bottom. There is the pit of self-doubt and the pit of despair. There is the pit of weariness. There are pits of loneliness and depression. We can also fall into a pit of anger, resentment or bitterness.

Whatever pit you are in today, the LORD is faithful to lift you up. If you feel faint turn your thoughts to the LORD. Do not live your life in the pit. When you are down let your prayers go up. The LORD will bring you up out of the pit.

Manna Moment

Are you often in the same pit? Ask God for wisdom to recognize the danger signs around you before you fall.

Day 185: Gracious and Compassionate

I knew that you are a gracious and compassionate God, slow to anger and abounding in love, a God who relents from sending calamity.
—Jonah 4:2 (NIV)

The God we serve is full of grace and compassion. He understands us better than any person ever could. The compassion of God goes beyond empathy, which says "I feel what you feel." His compassion takes it a step further and says, "Not only do I understand how you feel, but I am going to take action to relieve your suffering." Because of His grace and compassion God sent His only Son to set the captives free.

The grace of God says, "Instead of giving you what you deserve, I am going to forget your sins and cover you with my love." In addition to God's grace and compassion we have his undying love for us. It never fails and nothing can separate us from His love. God is slow to get angry and His favor lasts for a lifetime. He takes great pleasure in us and rejoices over us with singing. Praise God!

Manna Moment

Think of a time when God's grace and compassion touched you in a special way. How did you feel? Tell someone about your encounter.

Day 186: Watch and Wait

But as for me, I watch in hope for the LORD, I wait for God my Savior; my God will hear me.

—Micah 7:7 (NIV)

When you speak to the LORD, His ear is open to hear your voice. Therefore, keep your hope in Him alive and active with the knowledge that God recognizes your voice and He will answer your call.

You may be waiting to get a new job or looking to receive a promotion. You could be waiting for a spouse or trying to conceive a baby. You probably want to see someone you care about accept Jesus Christ as their Savior. Whatever the set of circumstances, watch in hope and wait for the LORD to deliver. Be confident that He will answer. While you wait for God, notice all the wonderful works He is doing in your life and in the world around you.

Manna Moment

Thank God for hearing your voice. Watch for the answer. It is coming.

Day 187: The Goodness of the LORD

The LORD is good, a refuge in times of trouble. He cares for those who trust in Him.
— Nahum 1:7 (NIV)

The LORD is good! What does His goodness mean to you? The ability to open your eyes and see the dawn of a new day reflects the goodness of the LORD. As God takes particular care of all our needs He shows us His goodness.

The reality that God turns on the faucet of His everlasting love and it continuously gushes into our lives and hearts is evidence of His goodness. When we are in trouble we can seek Him and He will be our refuge, our safe haven. This is the goodness of the LORD. There is no doubt the LORD is good.

Manna Moment

How have you been blessed with the goodness of the LORD? Tell someone.

Day 188: Record the Vision

Then the LORD answered me and said, "Record the vision and inscribe it on tablets, that the one who reads it may run. For the vision is yet for the appointed time; It hastens toward the goal, and it will not fail. Though it tarries, wait for it; For it will certainly come, it will not delay."

—Habakkuk 2:2-3 (NAS)

What are you believing God for today? Write down the vision the LORD has put on your heart. What will it look like when it has come to fruition? What or who will receive the benefits? It is very important to have something to strive for. Vision gives you direction and keeps you going. God will fulfill your vision at the appointed time. It will come to pass. Do all that is in your power to bring it about and then patiently wait on the LORD.

Manna Moment

Write down the vision you have for the rest of your life. Seek direction and help from the LORD to make it a reality.

Day 189: God Is with You

"The LORD your God is with you, he is mighty to save. He will take great delight in you, he will quiet you with his love, he will rejoice over you with singing."
— Zephaniah 3:17 (NIV)

Our God is not far off. He has not forgotten you. Our God is with you. He takes great delight in you. In other words, you are a source of pleasure to God. He enjoys fellowshiping with you, like He did with Adam and Eve when He walked in the Garden of Eden in the cool of the day. The LORD takes you in His arms and holds you close to His heart. His love wraps around you like a cozy blanket. He quiets you like a peacefully, sleeping baby. He sings over you like a mother does her newborn baby. God is with you.

Manna Moment

How does it feel to have the Creator of the universe rejoicing over you? What is your response?

Day 190: Be Strong and Work

"Be strong, all you people of the land," declares the LORD, *"and work. For I am with you,"* declares the LORD Almighty.
— Haggai 2:4 (NIV)

Be strong because the LORD is with you. He is your strength. He is the source of all life and power and His Spirit lives within you. He is with us even when our circumstances try to tell us He is not. He is always with us, even when we feel isolated from others. He is right there during our pity parties at which time we are entirely convinced that no one knows and no one cares what we are going through. Be strong and do the work He has for you. He will get you through the rest.

Manna Moment

What work has the LORD called you to? As you work, bear in mind the LORD is with you and you can draw from the strength He provides.

Day 191: Not By Might

"Not by might nor by power, but by my Spirit," says the LORD Almighty.
— Zechariah 4:6 (NIV)

It is not by our will, nor by our might, nor our power that anything of God is accomplished. It is by the Spirit of God that the battles of life are won. By His Spirit we are able to persevere through the storms. It is by the Spirit of God that lives are touched, inspired and healed. The Spirit of God gives us hope, strength and wisdom. May you live your life in accordance to the Spirit of God.

Manna Moment

Pray for the LORD Almighty to keep you full of His Holy Spirit and for you to make yourself fully available to His Spirit at all times.

Day 192: Never Changing

"I the LORD do not change."
—Malachi 3:6 (NIV)

The LORD does not change. He is the same today as He was yesterday and will be the same tomorrow.

The LORD loved you before you were born. The LORD loves you today and there is nothing you can do to make Him love you less. His love will never fail. The LORD had compassion on you in the past. The LORD has compassion on you now. The day you accepted His call to walk with Him is the day He poured His grace on you. And everyday you live His grace is available to you. The LORD is the only one we can depend on to remain the same. He does not change with the rising tide or alter His moods according to the position of the moon. We can count on Him to be all He ever was: loving, compassionate, gracious and forgiving.

Manna Moment

Can you think of anyone else in your life who has not changed? Thank the LORD for His stability.

Day 193: Wise Men and Women

After Jesus was born in Bethlehem in Judea, during the time of King Herod, Magi from the east came to Jerusalem and asked, "Where is the one who has been born King of the Jews? We saw his star in the east and have come to worship him."

—Matthew 2:1-2 (NIV)

Wise men and wise women still seek the King. Wisdom causes a person to make Jesus Christ the first priority in their life. Wisdom leads a person to seek His face, first and foremost, each and every day. He is the beginning and He is the end and without Him nothing exists. Let us strive to be wise men and women.

When the wise men saw the star they were overjoyed (Matthew 2:10). There is no greater joy than knowing King Jesus and fellowshiping with Him. Make sure you worship the King of kings throughout your day. May all we do and say bring honor and glory to His name.

Manna Moment

Do you seek the King on a daily basis? Make seeking Him your first priority every day.

Day 194: Healing Every Disease and Sickness

Jesus went throughout Galilee, teaching in their synagogues, preaching the good news of the kingdom, and healing every disease and sickness among the people.
—Matthew 4:23 (NIV)

When Jesus was on this earth in the flesh, He healed everyone. Jesus still heals. Our God is compassionate and He wants to make you whole. He has not forgotten about you. You are not an outcast. Jesus desires to bring healing to every heart and hope into every life. He brings healing where there is pain and brokenness in our lives.

Jesus is our great Physician. Be patient with Him. Doctor Jesus has an appointment marked on His calendar for you. God is working in you to conform you into His image, one of good health, holiness, love and wholeness. Praise to our God!

Manna Moment

Do you need physical healing? Does your heart need to be made whole by the great Physician? Tell the Lord where you need His healing touch in your life. Expect more from Him than you do your earthly doctor.

Day 195: Go the Extra Mile

If someone forces you to go one mile, go with him two miles.

—Matthew 5:41 (NIV)

As believers the Lord wants us to go above and beyond the expectations of others. We are not to skate through life doing the bare minimum. We are to pursue excellence in all we do.

As children of God our desire is to be like our heavenly Father. He goes the distance and then some. God does not just forgive our sins; He separates us from them, as far as the east is from the west. He does not just give us life; He gives us abundant life here on this earth and eternal life with Him in Heaven. He pours His blessings on us until our cups overflow.

Manna Moment

Think of a way you can go the extra mile with someone in your life. Put your plan into action.

Day 196: He Knows What You Need

But when you pray, go into your room, close the door and pray to your Father, who is unseen. Then your Father, who sees what is done in secret, will reward you. And when you pray, do not keep on babbling like pagans, for they think they will be heard because of their many words. Do not be like them, for

*your Father knows what you need before you
ask him.*
—Matthew 6:6-8 (NIV)

Our heavenly Father knows exactly what you need
before you open your mouth to ask Him. He knows
you better than you know yourself. He formed you in
your mother's womb and He knows how many hairs
you have on your head. He sees each tear that falls.
He knows your every need, whether it is physical,
emotional or spiritual. He is the God who will fulfill
your deepest need. Praise the LORD!

Manna Moment

What unmet needs do you have? Humble yourself and ask God to fulfill the need.

197: Forgiveness Is Liberating

*For if you forgive men when they sin against
you, your heavenly Father will also forgive
you. But if you do not forgive men their sins,
your Father will not forgive your sins.*
—Matthew 6:14-15 (NIV)

When we hold a grudge against someone we
are hurting ourselves more than we are hurting the
other person. It takes a lot of emotional energy to
hold onto a grudge. Holding onto offenses may cause
health problems as well as spiritual problems, like a
hardened heart. Liberate yourself. Let go of anything

you may be holding against someone else. It is more beneficial to forgive the other person and move forward with your life than to be stuck in a cesspool of negative energy, bitterness and resentment.

Forgiveness frees us to receive the forgiveness of God. Imagine that it takes both of your hands to hold a grudge, and Jesus comes to offer forgiveness. You are unable to take the forgiveness from Jesus unless you let go of the grudge you are holding. It is the same way with your heart. An unforgiving heart has no room to accept the forgiveness of God. When we let go of the offenses, true healing can begin and we can utilize our energy for something positive.

Sometimes we want to hold onto the hurt and pain and wear it like a badge. We walk around announcing to the world the wrongs we have suffered, so people pity us. What we must realize is that God knows our every hurt, pain and disappointment. Only He can bring the relief our heart longs for. God can turn around whatever happened to us and use it for good. So liberate yourself today and forgive those you need to forgive.

Manna Moment

Search your heart for a minute and see if there is someone you have not forgiven. Ask the Lord to help you forgive this person and move forward in your life.

198: Do Not Worry

"Therefore I tell you, do not worry about your life, what you will eat or drink; or about your body, what you will wear. Is not life more important than food, and the body more important than clothes?"

— Matthew 6:25 (NIV)

Do not worry about your life. Worry is a heavy load that God did not intend for us to carry. Our heavenly Father is aware of our needs: physical, spiritual and emotional, and He will provide. Keep putting Him first in all you do and He will supply anything you lack. You will eat and drink and be satisfied. The pains and hurts of your heart will be healed. Weariness will be replaced with energy and strength.

When the Lord is the center of your life, He will complete the circle of your life. Give thanks the Lord!

Manna Moment

When you start worrying about something, stop stressing out, write it down on a piece of paper, and ball it up. Toss it into a trashcan while saying, "I am putting this in Your hands Lord." If the situation comes back into your mind, say to yourself, "It is in the Lord's hands now." Then turn your thoughts toward past difficulties that God brought you through.

Day 199: Your Primary Concern

"Your heavenly Father already knows all your needs, and he will give you all you need from day to day if you live for him and make the Kingdom of God your primary concern. So don't worry about tomorrow, for tomorrow will bring its own worries. Today's trouble is enough for today."
—Matthew 6:32-34 (NLT)

When your primary concern is the Kingdom of God, you will have all you need from day to day. Once you make the Kingdom of God your primary concern, the two greatest commandments ever given will be your life's mission. Everything you do will focus on loving God with all of your heart, soul, mind and strength and you will love your neighbors as you love yourself.

Manna Moment

What are your major concerns today? Ask God to show you how you can resolve them and bring glory to the Kingdom of God at the same time.

Day 200: Ask, Seek and Knock

"Ask and it will be given to you; seek and you will find; knock and the door will be opened to you. For everyone who asks receives; he

who seeks finds; and to him who knocks, the door will be opened."
                                        —Matthew 7:7-8 (NIV)

Ask your heavenly Father for whatever you desire. James 4:2 tells us we do not have because we do not ask God. Moreover, we must ask with the right motives. As we continue to seek and search for truth, peace, love, a deeper relationship with Jesus, and His direction and guidance for our lives, we will find it.

Each time you present a desire to God in prayer, imagine yourself knocking on a door. When you knock on the door the Lord has for you, He will open it and you will receive.

Manna Moment

What is the number one desire of your heart? Ask God to bring it to pass. Seek His will. Watch for the door He opens. When God opens the door, go through it and receive what you have longed for.

Day 201: Solid Rock

"Therefore whoever hears these sayings of Mine, and does them, I will liken him to a wise man who built his house on the rock: and the rain descended, the floods came, and the winds blew and beat on that house; and it did not fall, for it was founded on the rock.

But everyone who hears these sayings of Mine, and does not do them, will be like a foolish man who built his house on the sand: and the rain descended, the floods came, and the winds blew and beat on that house; and it fell. And great was its fall."
—Matthew 7:24-27 (NKJ)

Be wise and build your life on the solid foundation of Jesus Christ. When troubles flood into your life and the winds of affliction beat on your house it shall not fall because you built it on Jesus, the solid Rock. When hardships blow into your life and trials pound on your rooftop, do not fear. You can withstand the pressure because you are standing on the solid Rock.

Anything else you choose to build your life on is shifting sand. Foolish men build their houses on the sand and experience total destruction. Their homes are unable to endure the storms of life and fall down.

Manna Moment

Look at a big rock and take note of its characteristics. It is not easily moved and it cannot be crushed. That is like our Rock, Jesus Christ. He is bigger than any problem that comes our way. He cannot be moved and He will not be crushed.

Day 202: Jesus Is Willing

A man with leprosy came and knelt before Him and said, "Lord, if you are willing, you can make me clean." Jesus reached out his hand and touched the man. "I am willing," he said. "Be clean!" Immediately he was cured of his leprosy.

—Matthew 8:2-3 (NIV)

Whatever you need, Jesus is willing to help you. His hand is stretched out toward you.

If you feel dirty, Jesus can make you clean. Be cleansed in the purifying flow of His blood. When you are sickly, He is the Great Physician. During times of weakness, He is a strong tower. In times of turmoil, He is the Prince of Peace. Allow Him to immerse your spirit and soul in His great peace. When you lack understanding, Jesus is the High Priest whose understanding has no limits. If it is forgiveness you are looking for, ask Him. Jesus Christ paid the price for all sins once and for all. He is faithful to forgive us of our sins when we confess them. Are you feeling unwanted and unloved? His love never fails.

Open your heart to the continual outpouring of His love. Jesus is the answer to every need. His hand is reaching out toward you and He is saying "I am willing."

Manna Moment

Kneel before the Lord and ask Him for what you need. Close your eyes and picture the hand of God reaching out to you. Reach out and take His hand.

Day 203: Great Faith

When Jesus had entered Capernaum, a centurion came to him, asking for help. "Lord," he said, "my servant lies at home paralyzed and in terrible suffering." Jesus said to him, "I will go and heal him." The centurion replied, "Lord, I do not deserve to have you come under my roof. But just say the word, and my servant will be healed."

When Jesus heard this, he was astonished and said to those following him, "I tell you the truth, I have not found anyone in Israel with such great faith."

Then Jesus said to the centurion, "Go! It will be done just as you believed it would." And his servant was healed at that very hour.
                    —Matthew 8:5-8, 10, 13 (NIV)

Faith pleases God. I encourage you to use the measure of faith you have and "great faith" will be developed within you. Trust in God with full confidence. Believe without a doubt, that all things are possible with God. As Jesus said, it will be done just as you have believed. When something or someone in your life is paralyzed, helpless, unable to move and in terrible suffering, go to Jesus with great faith. Believe that He is able and He will bring healing to your situation. Jesus is the miracle worker.

Manna Moment

What would you attempt to do if you knew that success was guaranteed? Ask God for great faith to do what He has put on your heart.

Day 204: He Touched Her

When Jesus came into Peter's house, he saw Peter's mother-in-law lying in bed with a fever. He touched her hand and the fever left her, and she got up and began to wait on him.

—Matthew 8:14-15 (NIV)

This passage of Scripture reflects the love and compassion of our Savior. Jesus cares. No matter how much we may doubt His presence in our lives, the truth of the matter is that He really cares. In the course of what Jesus was doing, He took the time to stop and touch Peter's mother-in-law and heal her. Can you imagine how she must have felt after Jesus touched her? Here she is lying in bed, suffering in pain, probably feeling pretty miserable and in walks Jesus. I am sure she had heard all the amazing stories people were telling about Him. Now she experiences His healing touch for herself, up close and personal.

The best way to experience Jesus is up close and personal. When we receive a touch from Jesus it brings healing and wholeness. Darkness leaves when we receive a touch from the Lord, the One who is light. Be receptive to a touch from the Lord today.

Manna Moment

Close your eyes and listen to your body. What part of your body needs a healing touch from Jesus? Is it your wounded heart? Is it your mind, overcome with anxious thoughts? Is there a part of your physical body that needs healing? Ask Jesus to touch you where you need it the most.

Day 205: Follow Him Wherever

When Jesus saw the crowd around Him, he gave orders to cross to the other side of the lake. Then a teacher of the law came to him and said, "Teacher, I will follow you wherever you go"
—Matthew 8:18-19 (NIV)

Jesus is looking for people who will follow Him wherever He goes. Are you willing to follow Jesus wherever He leads you? Will you walk in the footsteps of Jesus when the harsh winds of life blow in your face? Will you go along with Him when it is all you can do to put one foot in front of the other? Will you abide with Him when you do not understand why He is leading you in the opposite direction than you think you should be going?

Please know this with all your heart: God will not lead you to something that He will not bring you through! And after He leads you to that smooth, easy road of victory and success make sure Jesus can count on you to stick with Him and give Him all the glory.

Manna Moment

Is there an area of your life where you are consistently tempted to do things your own way? Ask God to soften your heart so that you are willing to follow His ways in this area.

Day 206: She Will Live

A ruler came and knelt before him and said, "My daughter has just died. But come and put your hand on her, and she will live." Jesus got up and went with him, and so did his disciples.
— Matthew 9:18-19 (NIV)

After the crowd had been put outside, he went in and took the girl by the hand, and she got up.
— Matthew 9:25 (NIV)

When Jesus Christ makes contact with someone who is dead, He infuses the breath of life into them.

John 10:10 in the New King James version tells us Jesus came in order for us to have life, and have it more abundantly. Jesus is all for a full, abundant life. His desire is for believers to grow and bear fruit.

Do you need a life-giving touch from Jesus right now? Is there something dead in your life or in your heart that needs a tender touch from Jesus to bring it back to life? Is there a part of your heart that has grown hard and cold to protect you from the cruel world? Jesus wants to place His hands on it and make it soft and warm again. Is there a seed of bitterness or unforgiveness buried deep within you that blocks the flow of compassion and love? Jesus would like to gently touch it and bring complete healing to this area of your life.

Once you are thoroughly awakened to His life flow you are able to receive His love and compassion fully. Do not let that which is dead, stay dead and begin to rot within you. Let the power that flows from the Master's hand resurrect that which is dead in your life. Live the full, abundant life Jesus Christ came to give us.

Manna Moment

Is there an area of your life that feels dead? Has so much life been drained out of you until you do not even dare to dream anymore? Ask the LORD to satiate your being with abundant life.

Day 207: Like Sheep Without a Shepherd

When he saw the crowds, he had compassion on them, because they were harassed and helpless, like sheep without a shepherd.
— Matthew 9:36 (NIV)

The crowds Jesus encountered as He went through towns and villages were like sheep without a shepherd, and He had compassion on them. When sheep have no shepherd, they are vulnerable to the attack of predators. At times our adversaries assault us nonstop. As soon as we get through one battle, another begins or we may even be engaged in several battles simultaneously.

We discover exactly how helpless we are in fighting this spiritual war when we fail to rely on the strength of Jesus Christ, our Shepherd. Our strength to endure the fight intensifies when we rely on the Lord. Instead of roaming through life harassed and helpless, like sheep without a shepherd, receive the compassion Jesus extends to you and follow Him. Live in His fold where Jesus, the good Shepherd watches over His flock and rescues His sheep. As a part of His flock, Jesus will guide you and shield you from harm.

Manna Moment

When you are being harassed and feeling helpless, look to the Lord for His care and concern. The compassion of Christ led Him to lay down His life for you. He has more than enough empathy to deliver you from the challenges you face.

Day 208: Do You Expect Someone Else?

When John heard in prison what Christ was doing, he sent his disciples to ask him, "Are you the one who was to come, or should we expect someone else?"
—Matthew 11:2-3 (NIV)

John the Baptist was locked up in prison for rebuking King Herod about having his brother's wife, among other evil things. John was put in jail for speaking the truth. Sitting in jail, he began to doubt and wonder if Jesus was the Messiah.

When you are imprisoned by the circumstances of your life, do you start to wonder if Jesus is the One? When things do not go according to your expectations, do you question God and His ability? No matter what happens in our lives, we must know in the core of our hearts that Jesus is the One. He is the One who sets the prisoners free, makes the blind to see and opens deaf ears. Jesus is the One whose tomb is empty because death could not confine Him. Do not look for another, because no one can compare to Him. Look for Jesus and believe that He is all you need.

Manna Moment

Is your natural inclination to look for the help of another person before you seek Jesus? Start a new habit of seeking Jesus first, in all situations.

Day 209: Come to Me

Then Jesus said, "Come to me, all of you who are weary and carry heavy burdens, and I will give you rest. Take my yoke upon you. Let me teach you, because I am humble and gentle, and you will find rest for your souls. For my yoke fits perfectly, and the burden I give you is light."
—Matthew 11:28-30 (NLT)

Are you weary? When you are drained, worn out and weighed down with burdens go to Jesus. Jesus calls us to come to Him. Give Him all your burdens and find rest for your soul. Your soul will rest peacefully in His tender loving care. He will take you out of the dry, barren land and lead you beside still waters and in green pastures.

The burden the Lord gives us is light and He knows us so well, it fits us perfectly. Each one of us has a different burden, but it is the one the Lord designed specifically for us and it is not heavy.

Manna Moment

What is the burden of your heart? You do not have to carry it any longer. Go to Jesus in prayer and give it to Him. After we learn from Him, the burden He gives us is light.

Day 210: Complete Restoration

Going on from that place, he went into their synagogue, and a man with a shriveled hand was there. Looking for a reason to accuse Jesus, they asked him, "Is it lawful to heal on the Sabbath?" He said to them, "If any of you has a sheep and it falls into a pit on the Sabbath, will you not take hold of it and lift it out? How much more valuable is a man than a sheep! Therefore, it is lawful to do good on the Sabbath." Then he said to the man, "Stretch out your hand." So he stretched it out and it was completely restored, just as sound as the other.

—Matthew 12:9-13 (NIV)

Think about the man with the shriveled hand. There is no indication of how long he had been in that condition, having a hand that was deformed and not fully functional. It is one thing to have a deformity that no one can see, but quite another to have it visible to everyone who looks at you. Chances are that he had even been teased. He probably tried to keep it hidden from the view of others as much as

234

possible. When Jesus drew the attention of the crowd to him, he probably felt a little uneasy, but Jesus wanted to bring wholeness into his life.

Do you have something in your life that is shriveled up, withered or dried up? Maybe you have been hurt by someone close to you and you let that part of your heart that cared so deeply for them shrivel up. Rather than risk being hurt again, you let that part of your heart wither away never to reach out again. If so, you need Jesus. He is the Lord of restoration. He restores things to function at their full capacity. We are valuable to Jesus and He wants us to be whole. Like the man in the synagogue, you may feel a little uneasy as you talk to the Lord about your shriveled up state but if you stretch it out before the Lord He will bring complete restoration into your life.

Manna Moment

Think about your life. Is there anything in you that is shriveled up? Is there an area of your life where you are not functioning at full capacity? If so, mark it down on a piece of paper. Describe what it feels like to be in that condition as long as you have. Take it to the Lord in prayer. Ask Him to bring complete restoration to that specific area of your life.

Day 211: Prayer Needed

Immediately Jesus made the disciples get into the boat and go on ahead of him to the other side, while he dismissed the crowd. After he

had dismissed them, he went up on a moun-
tainside by himself to pray. When evening
came, he was there alone . . .
    — Matthew 14:22-23 (NIV)

At the end of a long day, even Jesus had to get alone and pray. This habit is a great example for us to follow. No matter how long our task list, no matter what unexpected events get thrown our way, we should always, take the time to get alone with our heavenly Father and pray.

Remove any and all distractions and focus on Almighty God. Just talk to Him, heart to heart. Welcome prayer as a much needed release at the end of a busy day. He longs to hear your voice and fellowship with you.

Manna Moment

At the end of your day take some time to thank God for getting you through another day. Ask Him to help you see the current issues in your life through His eyes.

Day 212: In Trouble

Meanwhile, the disciples were in trouble far
away from land, for a strong wind had risen,
and they were fighting heavy waves. About
three o'clock in the morning Jesus came
to them, walking on the water. When the
disciples saw him, they screamed in terror,

thinking he was a ghost. But Jesus spoke to them at once. "It's all right," he said. "I am here! Don't be afraid."
> —Matthew 14:24-27 (NLT)

The disciples were in trouble and Jesus came to them. Sometimes, our lives are like being in a boat far away from land, in the midst of a storm. Whenever you find yourself in trouble, facing harsh winds of adversity and strong, violent waves are crashing down upon you, look for Jesus in the midst of the storm. Though it may seem that help is far away, Jesus is there. And He is speaking these same words to you, "It's all right. I am here! Don't be afraid."

You have to hold on and wait out the rough winds and turbulent waters until Jesus calms the storm or navigates you through it. He gives us the strength and endurance to withstand the most ferocious storms. He is good like that. He is always good.

Manna Moment

When you are fighting the heavy waves of life's storms and strong winds have risen up against you, focus on hearing the voice of the Lord. Jesus is saying, "It's all right. I am here! Don't be afraid." Jot these words down on an index card and read them out loud to yourself at least three times a day for as long as the storm rages around you.

Day 213: "Lord, Help Me!"

A Canaanite woman from that vicinity came to him, crying out, "Lord, Son of David, have mercy on me! My daughter is suffering terribly from demon-possession."
He answered, "I was sent only to the lost sheep of Israel." The woman came and knelt before him. "Lord, help me!" she said.
—Matthew 15:22, 24-25 (NIV)

We all need to come to Jesus and kneel before Him. On our knees before the Lord is one of the best places anyone could ever hope to be. When you open your eyes to a brand new day, fall to your knees and ask Jesus to help you get through the day. It is that simple.

Jesus tells us we need to come to Him like little children. Generally children do not have a problem asking for help. The more we realize we do not and cannot do it (our lives), by ourselves the better off we are. Be like the Canaanite woman and just say, "Lord, help me!" There is no shame in asking for help.

Manna Moment

What do you need help with? What are the needs of those around you? Kneel down before the Lord and ask for His help.

Day 214: A Dangerous Trap

*But Peter took him aside and corrected him.
"Heaven forbid, Lord," he said. "This will
never happen to you!" Jesus turned to Peter
and said, "Get away from me, Satan! You are
a dangerous trap to me. You are seeing things
merely from a human point of view, and not
from God's."*
　　　　　　　　　　—Matthew 16:22-23 (NLT)

In this Scripture, Peter is responding to Jesus
telling the disciples He had to go to Jerusalem where
He would be killed, and raised on the third day. Peter
did not see the phenomenal plan that God the Father
had already designed. Looking from a human point
of view, Peter could not fathom this extraordinary
plan that was going to bring salvation to the whole
world.

It is a dangerous trap to look at things merely
from a human point of view. From our limited,
earthly perspective things may look really dark and
dismal. We often get stuck down in the weeds, unable
to see anything clearly. However, God sees the big
picture from above. When we take off the shades of
our humanity and look through eyes of faith from
God's viewpoint we see a whole new picture. We
gain a much brighter outlook, once the light of God
illuminates the vision. During times of prayer be sure
to ask God to give you eyes of faith and the vision He
has for your life.

Manna Moment

Think of a situation that you thought was doomed. Recall how God worked it out. Give Him praise.

Day 215: Small as a Mustard Seed

"I tell you the truth, if you have faith as small as a mustard seed, you can say to this mountain, 'Move from here to there' and it will move. Nothing will be impossible for you."
—Matthew 17:20 (NIV)

Is there a mountain in your way today? A mountain is any huge problem you do not see how to get over or around. There are some mountains in life that Jesus wants us to climb, so we can exercise our faith muscles and gain strength. As we climb these mountains we learn endurance and perseverance. On the other hand, there are some mountains that God will just move if you speak to it in faith.

Mustard seeds are very small. Jesus tells us that all we need is a very, very small amount of faith to move mountains. Have faith in God. Have faith also in Jesus Christ, our Lord and Savior. Stand on the Word of God, full of confidence and tell your mountain to move. Believe God will do what you have asked.

Manna Moment

Visit a garden shop and see exactly how tiny a mustard seed is. Ask God to increase your faith, while you use the faith you have. Speak to your mountain.

Day 216: Like Little Children

And he said: "I tell you the truth, unless you change and become like little children, you will never enter the kingdom of heaven. Therefore, whoever humbles himself like this child is the greatest in the kingdom of heaven."

—Matthew 18:3-4 (NIV)

Jesus calls us to be like little children in order to enter the kingdom of heaven. Little children are humble. They are not ashamed or afraid to ask questions and expose their ignorance. Kids are teachable and always ready to learn. They also have big hearts. Little children love Mom and Dad unconditionally. Become like a little child in our Father's house.

Manna Moment

Observe little children at play. Notice their carefree, joyful spirits.

Day 217: Receive Your Sight

Two blind men were sitting by the road-side, and when they heard that Jesus was going by, they shouted, "Lord, Son of David, have mercy on us!"
Jesus stopped and called them. "What do you want me to do for you?" he asked. "Lord," they answered, "we want our sight." Jesus had compassion on them and touched their eyes. Immediately they received their sight and followed him.
—Matthew 20:30, 32-34 (NIV)

Are you emotionally or spiritually in the dark? Maybe confusion is clouding your vision. Perhaps anxiety is blocking your visibility. Whatever the case may be, Jesus has compassion for you. He is always asking you the question, "What do you want me to do for you (insert your name)?" If there is something that is blurring your vision today, ask Jesus to remove it and allow you to see clearly. After you receive your sight, make sure you continue to follow Him, just like the two blind men who received their sight.

Manna Moment

"What do you want Jesus to do for you?" Answer the question.

Day 218: Don't Let Your Love Grow Cold

*And many will turn away from me and betray
and hate each other. And many false prophets
will appear and will lead many people astray.
Sin will be rampant everywhere and the love
of many will grow cold. But those who endure
to the end will be saved.*
—Matthew 24:10-13 (NLT)

This passage of Scripture is part of a long description Jesus is giving about end times. Much of what goes on in our world today is a mirror image of what the Bible says will happen during end times. Some of the elements of end times are betrayal and hatred. Jesus says, sin will be rampant and the love of many will grow cold. In our modern day, where husbands kill their wives and unborn children, children kill their parents, and parents kill their children, it is safe to say that the love of many has grown cold.

Even though sin is rampant in our world, we must make sure our love does not grow cold. Cold love is harsh and has no concern for others. Someone whose love has grown cold can walk past others in dire need without even a thought of helping. When people sin against us it is easy to grow cold and full of hatred, however, Jesus calls us to love our enemies. An enemy could be a stranger such as a drunk driver who killed a loved one. An enemy could be someone close who betrayed us in some way. No matter what the case is, do not let your love grow cold. Stay at the feet of Jesus and there, your love will be kept warm.

At the feet of Jesus we can humble ourselves and instead of asking "Why me?" we can ponder "Why not me?" At the feet of Jesus we can open our hearts and receive His endless flow of love.

Manna Moment

Is there anyone you have allowed your love to grow cold toward? Ask Jesus to fill you with His warm love which gives life and covers sin.

Day 219: Keep Your Lamp Lit

"At midnight the cry rang out: 'Here's the bridegroom! Come out to meet him!' "Then all the virgins woke up and trimmed their lamps. The foolish ones said to the wise, 'Give us some of your oil; our lamps are going out.' " 'No,' they replied, 'there may not be enough for both us and you. Instead, go to those who sell oil and buy some for yourselves.' "But while they were on their way to buy the oil, the bridegroom arrived. The virgins who were ready went in with him to the wedding banquet. And the door was shut.
—Matthew 25:6-10 (NIV)

This parable illustrates the necessity and wisdom of being prepared for the return of Jesus because it will happen when people least expect it. Jesus forewarns His followers to "keep watch" and "be alert." Let us be prepared like the wise virgins. May we not let our lamps for the Lord go out, and block the work His Holy Spirit who dwells within us is performing.

Remain open to the flow of His power and love and your lamp will stay lit with the light Jesus gives. Listen and yield to the guidance of the Holy Spirit and He will prepare you for the circumstances that come your way. When your lamp is lit, you experience sweet fellowship with your Heavenly Father. Enter His Presence and enjoy the banquet He has for you, each and every day of your life. Praise God!

Manna Moment

Light a candle and let it burn during your prayer time. Let the flames serve as a reminder to keep a flame going in your heart for the Lord.

Day 220: According to Ability

"Again, it will be like a man going on a journey, who called his servants and entrusted his property to them. To one he gave five talents of money, to another two talents, and to another one talent, each according to his ability. Then he went on his journey."
—Matthew 25:14-15 (NIV)

In the above Scripture, Jesus is telling a parable that relates the Kingdom of Heaven to a man going on a trip, entrusting his property to his servants and returning after a long time to settle accounts. Similar to the man in the parable, Jesus gives to each person according to their own ability. He does not make excessive or unrealistic demands on us. He does not expect more than we have the potential to produce.

We all have God given talents, gifts and resources that we are to use to fulfill our purpose. He wants us to use them, not bury them in the ground like one of the servants in the parable. God also gives to each person a measure of faith. When we exercise our faith and work to develop our talents we realize the passion of our hearts and our dreams can become reality.

Manna Moment

What ignites the passion inside of you? Are you using that passion and your talents to accomplish the dream God put in your heart? If not, what is holding you back?

Day 221: A Solitary Place

Very early in the morning, while it was still dark, Jesus got up, left the house and went off to a solitary place, where he prayed.
—Mark 1:35 (NIV)

If Jesus, the Son of God Himself needed to start the day with prayer, how much more do we, being mere mortals, need to begin the day in prayer to our heavenly Father. We need a solitary place where there will be no interruptions or distractions. We need someplace where we can be still and enjoy fellowship with the LORD. A time of silence will help us hear His still small voice when He speaks to us.

As we seek to cultivate a more intimate relationship with our Father, let us develop the daily habit of spending time enveloped in a sanctuary of solitude, where we shut the world out and invite God in. Before your day gets started and you find yourself tangled up in traffic and fighting feelings of frustration, sneak away to a solitary place and spend some time talking and listening to your heavenly Father.

Manna Moment

If you do not have one, find a special place to spend exclusive time alone with the LORD. It should be a place that evokes feelings of relaxation. It can be indoors or outside as long as it is quiet and peaceful. Claim it as your own private corner of the world.

Day 222: Dine With the Lord

When the teachers of the law who were Pharisees saw him eating with the "sinners" and tax collectors, they asked his disciples: "Why does he eat with tax collectors and 'sinners'?" On hearing this, Jesus said to them, "It is not the healthy who need a doctor, but the sick. I have not come to call the righteous, but sinners."

—Mark 2:16-17 (NIV)

Jesus calls all sinners to Himself. He wants anyone who has ever sinned to come to Him and confess their sins. According to Romans 3:23, we have all sinned and fallen short of the glory of God. Jesus wants us to turn away from our sins and toward Him. His desire is for us to seek Him as desperately as a sick person seeks a doctor. And, like a physician, Jesus brings healing and wholeness to all who come to Him.

The Lord prepares a table before us. He longs for us to sit down with Him, to get comfortable and to eat a meal. In other words, He desires for us to set aside some time to fellowship with Him. He wants us close to Him, face to face. Dine with the Lord today and make reservations to be at His holy table every day.

Manna Moment

Close your eyes and imagine Jesus sitting across the table from you. The banquet table is heaped with heavenly delights. Now talk to Him about your day, as you enjoy your spiritual meal. Confess your sins to Him and praise Him for all the good things.

Day 223: Jesus Calms the Storm

Now when they had left the multitude, they took Him along in the boat as He was. And other little boats were also with Him. And a great windstorm arose, and the waves beat into the boat, so that it was already filling. But

He was in the stern, asleep on a pillow. And they awoke Him and said to Him, "Teacher, do You not care that we are perishing?"

Then He arose and rebuked the wind, and said to the sea, "Peace, be still!" And the wind ceased and there was a great calm.
—Mark 4:36-39 (NKJ)

The disciples panicked because the storm threatened to destroy them, and Jesus seemed unaware and unconcerned. The same power Jesus used to calm the storm is available to help us deal with the problems we face today. Think about the storms raging in your life – the situations that cause you much anxiety. Some storms seem like they will last forever. The dark clouds loom and the harsh winds knock us off our feet. The water floods in and we begin to believe God cannot or will not work in our situation.

When you are in the midst of the storm, you have two options: You can worry and assume that Jesus no longer cares, or you can refuse to give in to fear, and put your trust in Him. When you feel stressed or fearful, declare your need for God and then trust Him to calm the storm. God controls both the storms of nature and the storms of the troubled heart.

Manna Moment

Think of a time in your life when you felt Jesus was sleeping or did not care that you were perishing. Recall how the Lord brought you through this trying time and praise Him for it.

Day 224: Do Not Be Afraid, Only Believe

*And behold, one of the rulers of the syna-
gogue came, Jairus by name. And when he
saw Him, he fell at His feet and begged him
earnestly, saying, "My little daughter lies at
the point of death. Come and lay Your hands
on her, that she may be healed, and she will
live."*

—Mark 5:22-23 (NKJ)

*...Some came from the ruler of the syna-
gogue's house who said, "Your daughter is
dead. Why trouble the Teacher any further?"
As soon as Jesus heard the word that was
spoken, He said to the ruler of the synagogue,
"Do not be afraid; only believe."*

*Then He took the child by the hand,
and said to her, "Talith, cumi," which is
translated, "Little girl, I say to you, arise."
Immediately the girl arose and walked...*

—Mark 5:35, 26, 41-42 (NKJ)

When Jairus received the devastating news
that his daughter was already dead, fear must have
flooded his soul. In all probability, his throat immediately became parched. Most likely, his knees began
to tremble. Jesus, sensing his dread and despair, said
to him, "Do not be afraid; only believe." The Lord
helped Jairus let go of fear and focus on his faith.
Jesus ignited sparks of hope in the heart of Jairus.

When confronted with situations that cause us to fear, we too, must turn our attention away from the distressing news and put it on Jesus. We must listen to the words of Jesus and believe, believe in Him and believe that He is able to overcome any challenge we face.

Manna Moment

What brings fear to your heart? Have you ever received a doctor's report that flooded your soul with fear? Has the report of harm coming to a loved one filled you with panic? When terror seizes your heart, Jesus speaks the same words to you, "Do not be afraid; only believe."

Day 225: Get Some Rest

The apostles gathered around Jesus and reported to him all they had done and taught. Then, because so many people were coming and going that they did not even have a chance to eat, he said to them, "Come with me by yourselves to a quiet place and get some rest."

—Mark 6:30-31 (NIV)

In our hurried society and full schedules getting some rest never seems to make it on our plan of the day. Once we start the day we find ourselves bombarded with a never ending list of demands on our time and energy. Many of us frantically rush around from one event to another, barely getting a chance to stop and eat, let alone rest. We have become quite accustomed to this fast paced way of life, but eventually it catches up with us and we find ourselves entirely exhausted. Or we may feel like we are about to lose our sanity.

In order to maintain our good sense and keep ourselves from total burn out we must get away with Jesus, in a quiet place and get some rest. Not only do our bodies need rest but our minds need rest as well. We need to stop, take a deep breath and relax. Enjoy some well deserved rest in the presence of Jesus Christ, our good Shepherd.

Manna Moment

Go with Jesus by yourself to a quiet place and get some rest.

Day 226: Jesus Leads the Way

They were on their way up to Jerusalem, with Jesus leading the way, and the disciples were astonished, while those who followed were afraid.

—Mark 10:32 (NIV)

This Scripture illustrates the necessity of us allowing Jesus to lead the way. As we walk the walk of faith we must remember to get out of the way and follow Jesus wherever He leads us.

Mark 10:32 also shows us that even though some people followed Jesus, they were still afraid. Even on the journey of following Jesus, we may find there are times when fear gets the best of us. Fear of the future and what it holds. Fear of attempting something great and failing. Just remember, Jesus will get there before you and prepare the way for you. Even if you are fearful of what may come let Jesus lead the way and follow Him.

Manna Moment

Take a walk today and imagine yourself following Jesus. Notice the peace you experience when you let Jesus lead the way.

Day 227: Came to Serve

"Whoever wants to be a leader among you must be your servant, and whoever wants to be first must be the slave of all. For even I, the Son of Man, came here not to be served but to serve others, and to give my life as a ransom for many."
—Mark 10:43-45 (NLT)

Jesus is the perfect example of a true servant. He came to this earth to serve others and that is exactly what He did. He was continuously healing the sick, curing those with leprosy, giving the blind their sight, feeding the hungry, teaching the disciples and the crowds, healing the crippled, driving evil spirits out of the demon-possessed, making the deaf able to hear, raising the dead, preaching the good news and saving the lost. He was the greatest servant when He hung on the cross and gave His life for all of humanity.

May we emulate the Son of Man, Jesus Christ, and fervently serve others. No matter what our current condition, there is always someone we can serve in some way. Perhaps someone with no transportation needs a ride or a lonely person just needs someone to come and visit them and let them know the world has not forgotten about them. The possibilities are endless because people need each other.

Manna Moment

Think of a person who could benefit from your services today. If you cannot think of anyone, call your church or the nearest hospital or elderly care facility. Be the hands and feet of Jesus while you reach out and touch someone with an act of kindness.

Day 228: Are You Blinded?

Now they came to Jericho. As He went out of Jericho with His disciples and a great multitude, blind Bartimaeus, the son of Timaeus, sat by the road begging. And when he heard that it was Jesus of Nazareth, he began to cry out and say, "Jesus, the Son of David, have mercy on me!"…

Then they called the blind man, saying to him, "Be of good cheer. Rise, He is calling you." And throwing aside his garment, he rose

and came to Jesus. So Jesus answered and said to him, "What do you want me to do for you?" The blind man said to Him, "Rabboni, that I may receive my sight." Then Jesus said to him, "Go your way; your faith has made you well." And immediately he received his sight and followed Jesus on the road.
—Mark 10:46, 47, 49-52 (NKJ)

While we do not suffer a physical blindness, like Bartimaeus, there are times when we are spiritually blinded. Sometimes we walk around in a thick fog, unable to see the path the Lord wants us to take. We are possibly blinded by doubt and confusion. Weeds from the enemy grow over our path and obstruct our ability to see. We cannot see Jesus but we know He is there. We faintly hear His voice, from a distance. At times like this we must cry out to the Lord from the depths of our being. Jesus will hear your cry and draw you to Himself. Once you are in the arms of Jesus, He will respond to your need and clear the obstacles from your path. The fog will lift and you will see things clearly. Then you can be like Bartimaeus and follow Jesus. He is the Way (John 14:6).

Manna Moment

Has doubt and confusion caused you to blindly stumble around in a fog? Are you searching for some visibility from the Lord and what direction He wants you to take? Ask the Lord to open your eyes so you can see Him and follow Him as He shows you the way.

Day 229: Moving Mountains

"Have faith in God," Jesus answered. "I tell you the truth, if anyone says to this mountain, 'Go throw yourself into the sea,' and does not doubt in his heart but believes that what he says will happen, it will be done for him."
—Mark 11:22-23 (NIV)

What mountains do you need moved today? Mountains of disappointment, heartache or fear can loom so large before us that Jesus fades into the background of our lives. While sitting in the shadow of our cold, dark mountain, we can turn to the words of Jesus.

In Mark 11:24-25, Jesus teaches us to ask in prayer, believe we have received and forgive anyone we need to forgive. That is our part. When we do our part, God will do His part and the mountain will be moved. The mountain moving will be done for us when we believe and trust in God. So we can stop exerting all of our energy trying to push our mountain out of the way. Instead, we can get our eyes focused back on Jesus. He will move the mountain and make a way for us.

Manna Moment

Is there a mountain standing in between you and your desired destination? Say to your mountain "Go throw yourself into the sea." Believe in your heart and it will be done.

Day 230: Follow Closely

They took Jesus to the high priest, and all the chief priests, elders and teachers of the law came together. Peter followed him at a distance, right into the courtyard of the high priest. There he sat with the guards and warmed himself at the fire.
—Mark 14:53-54 (NIV)

Following Jesus at a distance was the beginning of Peter's downfall. Later on Peter went on to deny three times, that he was with Jesus. It is easy to get distracted and lose our focus when we follow Jesus at a distance. It is more advantageous for us to follow Jesus closely. He will lead the way, but we need to stay close to Him. We must not allow ourselves to get sidetracked and end up in a totally different place from the Lord.

Our God is an intimate God. He is there to catch every tear that falls. He wants us near Him, with no walls or barriers. He likes to fellowship with us. In Revelation 3:20, He invites us to open the door so He can come in and eat with us. In Matthew 10:28, Jesus invites those who are weary and burdened to come to Him. Psalm 140:13 tells us that the upright shall dwell in the presence of the LORD. As long as we stay close to the Lord, we will stay on the right path, because He will always lead us in the right direction. So make sure you follow the Lord closely.

Manna Moment

Think of the times you felt really close to the Lord? Were you engaging in daily quiet time with the Lord, humbling yourself before Him, confessing your sins and seeking His will? Participating in these activities consistently will ensure you maintain a close relationship with Him.

Day 231: Nothing is Impossible

"For nothing is impossible with God."
—Luke 1:37 (NIV)

Nothing is impossible with God. Be strong even when you cannot see the way out of a bad situation. All things are possible when you are walking with God. When the doctor gives you a bad report, when the bills are more than the income, when your children stray away from the Lord, when your marriage is on rocky grounds, when things are not going your way, stand on the Word of God.

It is possible for you to be healed. It is possible for God to meet all of your needs. It is possible for your children to be like the prodigal son and come back to the Lord. It is possible for your marriage to be on stable ground and for spouses to enjoy, love and respect each other. It is possible for you to have success in all you do. If God says it is possible, it is mission possible. His Word stands forever. Remember: Nothing is impossible with God.

Manna Moment

What seemingly impossible situation are you facing right now? Find a scripture that supports your victory in these circumstances and quote it until the Lord makes it a reality.

Day 232: He Has Been Mindful

And Mary said: "My soul glorifies the Lord and my spirit rejoices in God my Savior, for he has been mindful of the humble state of his servant. From now on all generations will call me blessed, for the Mighty One has done great things for me – holy is his name."
—Luke 1:46-49 (NIV)

The Lord has been mindful of you. He is well aware of your current condition, even if it seems like He may have forgotten you. He has done great things for you in the past and He will continue to do great things for you in the future. No matter what issues you are dealing with today, keep on trusting in the Lord. The Mighty One has you on His mind and He will work it out. May you glorify the Lord and rejoice in God our Savior for His great faithfulness.

Manna Moment

What great thing are you waiting for the Lord to perform? Lift it up to Him in prayer today.

Day 233: Thorns and Weeds

The seed that fell among the thorns stands for those who hear, but as they go on their way they are choked by life's worries, riches and pleasures, and they do not mature. But the seed on good soil stands for those with a noble and good heart, who hear the word, retain it, and by persevering produce a crop.
—Luke 8:14-15 (NIV)

Do not allow the worries of this life to choke the Word of life out of you. Pull the weeds of anxiety, frustration, discouragement, fear, bitterness, and unforgiveness out of the garden of your heart. Watch out for the thorns whose prick may lure you into seeking the riches and pleasures of this world and distract you from seeking our Lord and His will. Let the Master Gardener tend to your vine and make it bear more fruit. He brings forth fruit of love, joy, peace, self-control and gentleness. Persevere through the worries of this life and produce a bountiful crop.

Manna Moment

Pray to the Lord for His Word to fall on the good soil of your heart and for it to produce a crop. Ask Him for strength to persevere.

Day 234: Jesus Still Heals

Now a woman, having a flow of blood for twelve years, who had spent all her livelihood on physicians and could not be healed by any, came from behind and touched the border of His garment. And immediately her flow of blood stopped. And Jesus said, "Who touched Me?"

...Now when the woman saw that she was not hidden, she came trembling; and falling down before Him, she declared to Him in the presence of all the people the reason she had touched Him and how she was healed immediately. And He said to her, "Daughter, be of good cheer; your faith has made you well. Go in peace."

—Luke 8:43-45, 47-48 (NKJ)

This woman suffered for twelve years, putting her trust in man and depleting all of her resources. How many years have you suffered? How long have you carried around hurt and pain and held onto fears and anxieties, letting them deplete your inner resources?

As an encouragement, I implore you to grab a hold of the garment of Jesus. Push in, touch Him, and draw power from Him. Let the King of glory and the Lord of all, make you whole from the inside out. Have faith in the person of Jesus Christ to believe that just touching the edge of His garment will be life changing. We are needy people. We all have needs and Jesus understands them. Fall down at His feet, and tell Him the whole truth, your whole truth. Trust Him to heal you.

Manna Moment

Is there an issue in your life that is the source of suffering for you? How long has this challenge been plaguing you? Press in toward the Lord and fall down before Him. Tell Him the reason you need a healing touch from Him today.

Day 235: See His Glory

Two men, Moses and Elijah, appeared in glorious splendor, talking with Jesus. They spoke about his departure, which he was about to bring to fulfillment at Jerusalem. Peter and his companions were very sleepy, but when they became fully awake, they saw his glory and the two men standing with him.
—Luke 9:30-32 (NIV)

May we be fully awakened from our apathy, weariness, and depression so we can see the Lord in all of his glory. The whole world is full of His glory (Isaiah 6:3). His glory radiates throughout the earth, which He formed with His very own hands. The frosty mountain peaks and the dark valleys, the bare desert and the woods clothed with trees, all attest to the glory of the Lord. His glory can be seen in the wide variety of plants and animals He created, in myriads of colors, shapes and sizes.

We let the light of His glory shine through us as we walk according to His Holy Spirit. May we remove any obstacles in our lives that keep us from clearly seeing our glorious Lord. Eliminate all obstructions that hinder you from capturing the vision of our magnificent Lord and Savior, Jesus Christ in all of His glory.

Manna Moment

Take a walk and notice the glory of God all around you. Watch the sunrise as it lights up the sky. Listen to the beat of the waves crashing on the shore. Feel the wind as it brushes gently across your cheek. Look at the night sky twinkling with stars.

Day 236: Sit at His Feet and Listen

As Jesus and his disciples were on their way, he came to a village where a woman named Martha opened her home to him. She had a sister called Mary, who sat at the Lord's feet listening to what he said. But Martha was distracted by all the preparations that had to be made.

—Luke 10:38-40 (NIV)

Do not allow yourself to be distracted by endless preparations and concerns for the things of this world. There will always be something that needs to be washed, rinsed, dried, cleaned, polished, vacuumed, set up or taken down. Choose that which is better, to sit at the Lord's feet and listen to His voice, like Mary.

Listen to what the Holy Spirit speaks to your heart as you read His Word. Jesus said His sheep listen to His voice (John 10:27), but you will have difficulty hearing His voice if you are distracted by other things.

Manna Moment

Sit in your favorite, most comfortable chair and ask the Lord to open your ears to hear His voice. Just sit and listen.

Day 237: Life Not in the Abundance of Possessions

Then he said to them, "Watch out! Be on your guard against all kinds of greed; a man's life does not consist in the abundance of his possessions."
—Luke 12:15 (NIV)

Jesus warns us to "Watch out!" We are to guard ourselves against getting caught in the snare of greediness. There are all kinds of greed. There is greed for power, status, control, or authority. There is also a greed for possessions, expensive cars, huge homes, the biggest and newest gadgets or other luxurious toys. Greed is insatiable. The more a person caught in the snare of greed gets the more they want. They experience no degree of contentment because they are trying to fill a void meant for the presence of Almighty God with their possessions. No matter what material goods we acquire in this life, they will never provide any lasting fulfillment, just a quick thrill at the moment of acquisition.

The things that really matter in this life are not measured by the amount of worldly goods we manage to collect. What really matters are the lives we touch with our love.

Manna Moment

Do you have an excessive drive to acquire material possessions? Ask God to help you be more passionate about seeking Him and loving others and less desirous of obtaining possessions.

Day 238: Eighteen Years of Infirmity

Now He was teaching in one of the synagogues on the Sabbath. And behold, there was a woman who had a spirit of infirmity eighteen years, and was bent over and could in no way raise herself up.

But when Jesus saw her, He called her to Him and said to her, "Woman, you are loosed from your infirmity." And He laid His

265

*hands on her, and immediately she was made
straight, and glorified God.*
—Luke 13:10 (NKJ)

Can you imagine what eighteen years of infirmity
must have been like for this woman? What a living
hell she must have experienced. Her situation was
much more intense than most of the things which
complicate our lives today. I wonder how many
times the devil whispered in her ear that God did not
love her. I wonder how many times she felt unloved
and uncared for. How many times did she feel alone?
How many days did she find herself totally depressed
and wanting to die just to put an end to the pain and
suffering? How many days did she wake up feeling
completely worthless and useless? In eighteen years,
how many times did she cry out to God saying, "How
long must I suffer, Lord?"

I encourage you to go the distance with God.
Many of us have been dealing with certain issues
for a number of years and we wonder, "How long,
God?" Everything will come together according to
His perfect time, just like it did for this woman. Her
day and time was, ordained by God.

Manna Moment

Do you have a longstanding problem that has
you spiritually bent over? Have you been unable to
raise yourself up? Ask Jesus to loose you from the
affliction.

Day 239: When We Stray

*Then He said: "A certain man had two sons.
And the younger of them said to his father,
'Father, give me the portion of goods that
falls to me.' So he divided to them his livelihood. And not many days after, the younger
son gathered all together, journeyed to a far
country, and there wasted his possessions
with prodigal living. But when he had spent
all, there arose a severe famine in that land,
and he began to be in want."*
—Luke 15: 11-14 (NKJ)

*"And he arose and came to his father. But
when he was still a great way off, his father
saw him and had compassion, and ran and
fell on his neck and kissed him.*
—Luke 15:20 (NKJ)

When we are looking at the thing God has said
"Thou shall not do," and pondering it in our heart, we
have strayed away from our heavenly Father and His
perfect will for us. When we wander off, God looks
for us and waits for us to stop being rebellious and
turn toward Him with a repentant heart, a heart that is
open to the will of God in all areas of our lives.

God loves us and has compassion on us. And
when we turn toward Him, He will run toward us
and embrace us in His loving arms. He will not judge
us or condemn us. He will rejoice over us.

Manna Moment

If you have strayed away from God, pray this prayer: "O heavenly Father, show me if there is any area of my life where I have taken my own path and not Yours. Please help me to return to You and give that area of my life and my heart over to You. In the name of Jesus Christ I pray. Amen."

Day 240: In Need

"Not long after that, the younger son got together all he had, set off for a distant country and there squandered his wealth in wild living. After he had spent everything, there was a severe famine in that whole country, and he began to be in need."
—Luke 15:13-14 (NIV)

How many times have we gone in the opposite direction of our heavenly Father to follow our own wishes or desires? How many times have we realized our true need after we got to the end result of what we thought we wanted? To be in need . . . in need of the Father's presence in our lives, where we have to call out, "God where are You?" To be in need, where deep within our souls we ache and our minds wonder if anyone really cares. Sometimes our need takes us to a place where we question if there is anyone who even understands our plight. At other times our need takes us to a place where we hunger and thirst for a touch from our God and Father to let us know that He is thinking about us and has not forgotten us.

In our hour of need, may we be like the prodigal son who came to his senses and returned to his father's house (Luke 15:17-20). May we return to our Father's house, the place where His glory dwells. Return to the place where He longs to hold you close to Him and surround you with His love and His compassion. He longs to embrace you and whisper in your ear, "Everything is going to be all right. I am here. Do not be afraid. Do not be dismayed."

Manna Moment

Are you "in need" today? Return to your Father's house and He will meet all of your needs.

Day 241: Cry Out Day and Night!

Then Jesus told his disciples a parable to show them that they should always pray and not give up. He said: "In a certain town there was a judge who neither feared God nor cared about men. And there was a widow in that town who kept coming to him with the plea, 'Grant me justice against my adversary.'

"For some time he refused. But finally he said to himself, 'Even though I don't fear God or care about men, yet because this widow keeps bothering me, I will see that she gets justice, so that she won't eventually wear me out with her coming!"

And the Lord said, "Listen to what the unjust judge says. And will not God bring about justice for His chosen ones, who cry out to him day and night? Will he keep putting them off? I tell you, he will see that they get justice, and quickly. However, when the Son of Man comes, will he find faith on the earth?"

—Luke 18:1-8 (NIV)

In this parable Jesus encourages us to be consistent (being firm) and persistent in our praying. Do not lose hope in the circumstances you are dealing with. Cry out to God day and night. Being persistent means you continue on, with determination, in spite of the difficulties. Jesus asked an interesting question about faith at the end of this parable. "When the Son of Man comes, will he find faith on the earth?" Maybe He asked this question because it takes faith to always pray and not give up.

Listen to Jesus. Do not give up. Stop looking at your circumstances. Our heavenly Father will work out whatever concerns you. Open your ears and hear Jesus whispering to you, "Do not give up! I AM here with you."

Manna Moment

Is there a situation in your life that you have given up on? Cry out to the LORD day and night about it. Keep coming to Him with your plea. Will not God

bring about justice for you when you cry out to him
day and night?

Day 242: What Do You Want Him to Do For You?

*As Jesus approached Jericho, a blind man
was sitting by the roadside begging. When he
heard the crowd going by, he asked what was
happening. They told him, "Jesus of Nazareth
is passing by." He called out, "Jesus, Son of
David, have mercy on me!"*

*Jesus stopped and ordered the man to be
brought to him. When he came near, Jesus
asked him, "What do you want me to do for
you?" "Lord, I want to see," he replied. Jesus
said to him, "Receive your sight; your faith
has healed you." Immediately he received
his sight and followed Jesus, praising God.
When all the people saw it, they also praised
God.*

—Luke 18: 35-38, 40-43 (NIV)

The compassion of Jesus is always asking us,
"What do you want Me to do for you?" What an
awesome position we are in to have such a loving,
caring and compassionate Lord. He is our Shepherd
and He is concerned about our needs at all times.

Jesus has given us sight just like He did the blind
beggar. He has given us spiritual eyes to see Him.
Once we see Him we cannot help but love Him.
And letting the beggar serve as an example to us, we

should also follow Jesus and praise God. Wherever He leads us, we must stay on the narrow path and follow Him. And we can praise God for allowing us to see Him for who He really is, the Messiah, our Lord, Savior and King. Praise Him!

Manna Moment

Jesus asks you the same question: "What do you want Me to do for you?" Take some time to think about it and then respond to the Lord.

Day 243: If You Are Lost...

"For the Son of Man came to seek and to save what was lost."
          —Luke 19:10 (NIV)

If you are lost in sin, Jesus will forgive you.
If you are lost in sickness, Jesus brings healing.
If you are lost in fear and anxiety, Jesus gives you peace.
If you are lost in sorrow, Jesus fills your heart with joy.
If you are lost in discouragement, Jesus encourages you.
If you are lost in despair, Jesus gives you hope.
If you are lost in the darkness, Jesus is the light.
If you are lost in deception, Jesus is the truth.
If you are lost in weariness, Jesus will be your strength.

If you are lost in feelings of not being loved, Jesus
loves you more than His own life.

If you are feeling near death, Jesus gives you life
and life more abundantly.

If you are lost, Jesus is the Way, follow Him!

Manna Moment

How do you know when you are not lost? You
are walking with your hand in His and He is leading
you along on the path He has for you. You fully trust
in the Lord to provide for all your needs. You may
not know your final destination but you know as long
as you stick with Him, He will get you exactly where
you are supposed to be.

Day 244: Recognize the Time

*As he (Jesus) approached Jerusalem and saw
the city, he wept over it and said, "If you,
even you, had only known on this day what
would bring you peace- but now it is hidden
from your eyes. The days will come upon you
when your enemies will build an embank-
ment against you and encircle you and hem
you in on every side. They will dash you to
the ground, you and the children within
your walls. They will not leave one stone on
another, because you did not recognize the
time of God's coming to you."*

—Luke 19:41-44 (NIV)

May we not be like the people of Jerusalem. Let us recognize the time when God comes to us. Each day He is there waiting for us to acknowledge Him and fellowship with Him. He surrounds us with His love, every moment of the day. He uses our weakness to show His strength in our lives. May you recognize that our God is a mighty God, as you follow Him each and every day. It would be a tragedy not to recognize the time of God's coming to you.

Manna Moment

Realize that God comes to you any time of day. He is available twenty-four hours a day. As long as the breath of life is within you, take time to honor Him. Recognize that now is the time when He pours out His Spirit on men, women and children.

Day 245: Take Jesus at His Word

The royal official said, "Sir, come down before my child dies." Jesus replied, "You may go. Your son will live." The man took Jesus at his word and departed. While he was still on the way, his servants met him with the news that his boy was living.
— John 4:49-51 (NIV)

Do you take Jesus at His Word? The journey of faith requires us to take Jesus at His Word. He says that all things are possible with God (Mark 10:27). Therefore, we need to believe the seemingly impossible situation we face *is* possible with God on our side. If we take Jesus at His word in John 14:6, when He says, He is the way and the truth and the life, then we will follow Him at all times. In John 10:10 Jesus says, "I have come that they may have life, and have it to the full." Take Jesus at His word and live the full life that He promises to give us. Amen.

Manna Moment

Do you take Jesus at His word when difficulties arise in your life? Commit the words of Mark 10:27 to memory: all things are possible with God. Speak it out when trying times come.

Day 246: Do You Want To Be Made Well?

After this there was a feast of the Jews and Jesus went up to Jerusalem. Now there is in Jerusalem by the Sheep Gate a pool, which is called in Hebrew, Bethesda, having five porches. In these lay a great multitude of sick people, blind, lame, paralyzed, waiting for the moving of the water. For an angel went down at a certain time into the pool and stirred up the water; then whoever stepped in first, after the stirring of the water, was made well of whatever disease he had. Now a certain man was there who had an infirmity thirty-eight years. When Jesus saw him lying there, and knew that he already had been in

> *that condition a long time, He said to him,*
> *"Do you want to be made well?"*
> —John 5:1-6 (NKJ)

After thirty-eight years, this man's problem had become a way of life. According to John 5:7, he replied, he had no one to help him get into the pool. He probably had no hope of ever being healed, no hope of ever receiving the help he needed. I imagine there were many times in those thirty-eight years this man may have felt that God was punishing him for something or that his situation was hopeless. I imagine there were several times in those thirty-eight years that he pleaded with God to let him die. Maybe you can relate to being in such utter despair that you feel like just "laying there."

No matter how trapped you feel in your current situation, God can minister to your deepest needs, to your every need. You do not have to wait for the moving of the water. Jesus is here for you right now, asking, "Do you want to be made well?" Do not let a problem or hardship cause you to lose hope. God has a special work for you to do in spite of your condition or circumstance, or even because of it.

Manna Moment

Have you been afflicted with an ailment for a number of years? Do you want to be made well? Accept no more excuses about why things are the way they are. Beseech the Lord to set you free from whatever ails you.

Day 247: I Can Do Nothing by Myself

*"By myself I can do nothing; I judge only as
I hear, and my judgment is just, for I seek not
to please myself but him who sent me."*
— John 5:30 (NIV)

If Jesus admits He can do nothing by Himself,
why do we have such a hard time admitting we can
do nothing on our own? We need God and we also
need other people. No matter how long we stay in
denial, this simple truth will not change. It is okay
to admit we need other people. Back in the Garden
of Eden, God decided it was not good for man to
be alone, Genesis 2:18. He created us to experience
relationships with other people. Together, believers
make up the body of Jesus Christ.

It is wise to acknowledge our need for God. In
order to have real success in life, we must rely on our
heavenly Father, request His assistance and follow
His direction. Let us be like Jesus and seek to please
our Father.

Manna Moment

Are you currently involved in a project you could
use some help with? Find someone who has the skills
and assets you need, and ask for help. When you
find the right person, you can seek God together and
solicit His help.

277

Day 248: Are You Thirsty?

*On the last day, that great day of the feast,
Jesus stood and cried out, saying, "If anyone
thirsts, let him come to Me and drink. He who
believes in Me, as the Scripture has said, out
of his heart will flow rivers of living water."*
—John 7:37-38 (NKJ)

Are you thirsty? Drink in the goodness of the
Lord. Drink in, His mercy and His grace. Partake of
His everlasting love for you and let it permeate your
entire being. Drink in, the forgiveness of the Lord.
Let His forgiveness wash away all shame and guilt.
Drink in, the strength of the Lord. If you are thirsty
for peace, drink from the Lord's cup. His cup is calm
and tranquil.

May the Lord pour out His love, peace and joy on
you until rivers of living water flow out of your heart
and touches everyone He brings your way.

Manna Moment

Are you thirsting for more out of life? Only Jesus
can satisfy your thirsty soul. Go to Jesus as often as
you like and let Him fill your cup until it overflows.

Day 249: Follow the Light

*… "I am the light of the world. Whoever
follows me will never walk in darkness, but
will have the light of life."*

"I have come into the world as a light, so that no one who believes in me should stay in darkness."
—John 8:12; 12:46 (NIV)

As long as we follow Jesus we have the light of life. As we wander away from Jesus and the path that He is trying to lead us on, the light gets dimmer and dimmer. The farther away we go the more difficult it becomes to stay focused on Jesus. By the time we realize we cannot see the light anymore we are in utter despair. The darkness has overcome our soul and we are overwhelmed with all that life brings our way. Once we are in the darkness, sadness, anger, bitterness, resentment, depression, apathy, loneliness, anxiety or self-pity begins to invade our minds and our emotions. It can leave us feeling completely defeated.

This is when we need to run back to Jesus and seek out His light. Jesus is our joy. Jesus is our peace. Jesus is our life. Follow the light. Stay on the path with Him; hold onto His hand as He leads you step by step. Keep your eyes on Him and follow every step He takes.

Manna Moment

Are you following the light of the world? If you believe in Jesus you do not have to stay in darkness. With each step you take, ask yourself, "Am I moving toward the light or away from the light?"

Day 250: Set Free by the Truth

Jesus said, "If you hold to my teaching, you are really my disciples. Then you will know the truth, and the truth will set you free."
—John 8:31-32 (NIV)

Jesus is the truth and He sets us free (John 14:6). Jesus sets us free from all our pain and fears. We are free from the chains of the past. Free from guilt and self-condemnation. Free from any chains attempting to hold us back. When you feel imprisoned by doubt, confusion, sadness, depression, or frustration, remember the LORD sets the prisoners free (Psalm 146:7). We are free as an eagle to fly toward God and what He has planned for us.

Manna Moment

In order for the truth to set us free, we have to know the truth. Commit to studying the Word of God on a consistent basis. If possible, join a Bible study group or class.

Day 251: The Good Shepherd

The man who enters by the gate is the shepherd of his sheep. The watchman opens the gate for him, and the sheep listen to his voice. He calls his own sheep by name and leads them out. When he has brought out all his

*own, he goes on ahead of them, and his sheep
follow him because they know his voice.*
—John 10:2-4 (NIV)

Jesus is the good Shepherd (John 10:11). We are
His sheep. Because of the great love He has for us,
the good Shepherd lays down his life for the sheep.
Jesus knows His sheep. He calls each one of us by
name. He leads us beside quiet waters and restores
our soul (Psalm 23:2-3). We are in the hand of the
good Shepherd and no one can snatch us out (John
10:28). Listen for the voice of the Good Shepherd…
quietly and gently He calls you by name.

Manna Moment

Take a few minutes to sit and listen for the voice
of the good Shepherd. Seek to know Him more each
day, as you journey together.

Day 252: Abundant Life

*"The thief does not come except to steal, to
kill, and to destroy. I have come that they
may have life, and that they may have it more
abundantly."*
—John 10:10 (NKJ)

Jesus came to give us abundant life. Abundant
life is peace flowing like a river in the depths of our
soul. Abundant life is joy, bubbling like a brook in
the crevices of our heart.

We experience a bountiful life when we completely trust and fully rely on Father God to meet all of our needs. We are living a plentiful life when we allow the love of Jesus to fill our very beings like a vessel until it spills over into the lives of others. The abundant life is a life that is yielded to the Holy Spirit and the work He is doing within. It is allowing the Holy Spirit to be our comforter and guide. He will lead us into all truth and that truth sets us free to enjoy the abundant life.

Manna Moment

Are you living the abundant life? If not, what is stopping you? Give it to God in prayer and jump into the abundant life Jesus has provided for you.

Day 253: Full Extent of His Love

It was just before the Passover Feast, Jesus knew that the time had come for him to leave this world, and go to the Father. Having loved his own who were in the world, he now showed them the full extent of his love.
After that, he poured water into a basin and began to wash his disciples' feet, drying them with the towel that was wrapped around him.
—John 13:1, 5 (NIV)

Jesus wants to show you the full extent of His love. Jesus wants to wash your feet. Will you sit by the basin of His love while He washes the dirt and grime of the world from you? He wants to wash away all discouragement, distress, hurt and bitterness. The water of His love will wash away all anxiety, disappointment and frustration. When He washes you, anger, pride, shame and guilt will fade away.

As He dries you with the towel of His grace, the light of His love will shine through you, and His glory will settle upon you. Then you will sparkle with His joy and His peace.

Manna Moment

Whose feet can you wash today? To whom can you show the full extent of your love? Provide for a needy person, feed a hungry person, clothe a naked person, or give shelter to a homeless person.

Day 254: Troubled Heart?

"Do not let your hearts be troubled. Trust in God; trust also in me."
—John 14:1 (NIV)

Is your heart troubled? Is it full of turmoil? When we trust in God and in His Son, Jesus, we experience true peace. To embrace Jesus we must let go of all the other "stuff" in our lives, all the other "junk" that weighs us down. We have to throw off everything that hinders us (Hebrews 12:1).

Once we do that, we are free to draw closer to God. The closer we are to Him the easier it becomes to put more of our trust in Him. As we allow His Presence to fill our heart we experience His peace. As His peace occupies more of your heart and mind, there is less room for anxiety and discouragement.

Manna Moment

Close your eyes and visualize your heart opening up to God and His Holy Spirit filling your heart. Sit quietly for a while and enjoy the serenity of His Holy Spirit.

Day 255: He Lives with You

"And I will ask the Father, and he will give you another Counselor to be with you forever – the Spirit of truth. The world cannot accept him, because it neither sees him nor knows him. But you know him, for he lives with you and will be in you."

—John 14:16-17 (NIV)

The Apostle Paul tells us in Ephesians 1:13 that having believed in Jesus we were marked in Him with a seal, the promised Holy Spirit, who is a deposit guaranteeing our inheritance. We have His Holy Spirit dwelling on the inside of us. The Holy Spirit is our Counselor who teaches us all things and guides us into all truth. The Holy Spirit helps us when we are weak and intercedes for us in our prayers to the Father. His Spirit lives with you.

May you submit to the leading and teaching of the Holy Spirit at all times.

Manna Moment

Ask the Father to make you sensitive to the presence of the Holy Spirit within you. Ask Him to help you follow His guidance and understand the truth as He reveals it to you.

Day 256: Grief Turns to Joy

I tell you the truth, you will weep and mourn while the world rejoices. You will grieve, but your grief will turn to joy. A woman giving birth to a child has pain because her time has come; but when her baby is born she forgets the anguish because of her joy that a child is born into the world.
　　　　　　　　　　　—John 16:20-21 (NIV)

Our present pain and suffering is like a woman giving birth. Our times of grieving will be forgotten when we enter into the fullness of what God has in store for us. The time we spend on this earth is like the blink of an eye compared to eternity, where we will experience everlasting joy. The day we step into eternity and see Jesus face to face, the pain and suffering we endured on this earth will not matter.

Take comfort in knowing that the pain and suffering we experience in this life is temporary and cannot be compared to the glory that is to be ours (Romans 8:18).

Manna Moment

Has there been a situation in your life where your grief was turned to joy? Praise God for it.

Day 257: Take Heart

"I have told you all this so that you may have peace in me. Here on earth you will have many trials and sorrows. But take heart, because I have overcome the world."
—John 16:33 (NLT)

Jesus equips us with the knowledge that we will have many trials and sorrows here on earth. And the apostle Peter wrote in 1 Peter 4:12, do not be surprised at the painful trial you are suffering. So we can expect to encounter various trials in the course of our lives. Regardless of the number of trials we confront or the depth of the sorrow we go through, we can rise above our circumstances and have peace in our Lord Jesus Christ.

May your heart be encouraged today as you remember that Jesus has overcome the world. In Him you have the victory. Praise God!

Manna Moment

What kinds of trials and sorrows do you face? Write Jesus in big letters across the top of a piece of paper. Under His name list the trials and sorrows you are currently dealing with in small letters. When you are finished, look at the paper and understand that Jesus Christ reigns over any problem you have. Let that perspective remain in the forefront of your mind.

Day 258: Complete the Work

"I have brought you glory on earth by completing the work you gave me to do."
—John 17:4 (NIV)

Let us be like Jesus and complete the work our heavenly Father has given us. This brings glory to God. May the work given to us by the LORD not be like many of our projects which get started and never finished. May parents complete the task of raising their children up in the way they should go. May husbands love their wives and wives love their husbands and complete the work of having a successful and happy marriage. When it comes to loving the Lord and loving our neighbors may we complete the work and give glory to God.

Manna Moment

What have you left undone? Have you made any promises and then did not complete them? If it was something the Lord put on your heart, then do it. Tie up all loose ends.

Day 259: Just Believe

A week later his disciples were in the house again, and Thomas was with them. Though the doors were locked, Jesus came and stood among them and said, "Peace be with you!" Then He said to Thomas, "Put your finger here; see my hands. Reach out your hand and put it into my side. Stop doubting and believe."

—John 20:26-27 (NIV)

Jesus is standing by your side today and He is saying to you, "Stop doubting, and believe." Blessed are those who have not seen and yet have believed (John 21:29). Believe in Him. Believe Him. Believe in the promises of God. Take Him at His Word. Believe that our God is bigger than any challenge you have. Nothing is too difficult for Him.

Manna Moment

What are you struggling to believe? Do you find it hard to believe that God loves you? Do you believe that He wants the best for you? Do you sometimes wonder how God is working for your good? Just believe.

Day 260: Times of Refreshing

Repent, then, and turn to God, so that your sins may be wiped out, that times of refreshing may come from the Lord,
—Acts 3:19 (NIV)

When we do anything against the will of God we have turned our backs to Him. We have decided we want to handle the situation our own way. During these times we need to repent or change directions. When we repent we turn away from our sin and toward God. When true repentance occurs, He wipes away our sin, as if it never happened. He separates us away from our sins as far as the east is from the west.

After we repent, we will experience a time of revitalization from the Lord. The phrase, "times of refreshing," sounds delightful. It is a time when your spirit, soul and body will be uplifted and energized. It is a time of renewal and exhilaration.

Manna Moment

Close your eyes. Take a deep breath in and exhale gently and slowly. Indulge in a fantasy of what a time of refreshing would be for you.

Day 261: No Other Name

Salvation is found in no one else, for there is no other name under heaven given to men by which we must be saved.

—Acts 4:12 (NIV)

Salvation is found in no one, but Jesus Christ of Nazareth. There is no other name by which we must be saved. Jesus sets us free from sin and death. Jesus is the only name we can call to receive the help we need. Jesus is the name we can call on in times of temptation and He provides a way of escape. The enemy of our soul trembles at the name of Jesus. The name of Jesus breaks the shackles that hinder us from experiencing abundant life. Jesus is the only name worthy of all our praise. Call on the name of the Lord and be saved. There is no other name.

Manna Moment

When you are confronted with difficulties what name do you call on first? A friend? Your Pastor? Seek the Lord first and foremost. Call on His name. Your help comes from the Lord.

Day 262: Fighting Against God?

"Therefore, in the present case I advise you: Leave these men alone! Let them go! For if their purpose or activity is of human origin, it will fail. But if it is from God, you will not

be able to stop these men; you will only find
yourselves fighting against God."
— Acts 5:38-39 (NIV)

In the above passage, the Pharisee named Gamaliel is warning the men of Israel not to mess with Peter and the other apostles. This scripture brings out a good point: What we try to do by sheer human will and in our own strength is destined for failure. At times we forge ahead trying to push our own agenda. If we try to force the issue in the flesh we will only find ourselves fighting against God. Who do you think will win that battle?

On the other hand, no man can stop what we do according to God's will and in the power of His Holy Spirit. When all is said and done, man cannot circumvent the plans of God.

Manna Moment

Are you fighting against God? Take a step back, re-evaluate the situation and seek God. Ask Him to reveal His will and purpose in the situation. Then, when you go forward no man will be able to stop you.

Day 263: Stoned and Left for Dead

The Jews from Antioch and Iconium came there; and having persuaded the multitudes, they stoned Paul and dragged him out of the city, supposing him to be dead.
— Acts 14:19 (NKJ)

Does life have you feeling like Paul, stoned, dragged and left for dead? Have you been hit with the stone of despair? Or did the stone of pain and hurt get you? Did the stone of criticism and negativity knock you off your feet? Have you been bruised by the stone of depression? Did the stone of betrayal or disappointment hit you unexpectedly in the back? Did the stone of fear come hurling at your head? Has the stone of fatigue zapped all your energy? Have you been dragged through conflict and adversity? Are you feeling abandoned, neglected and left for dead?

Read on. In Acts 14:20, it says that when the disciples gathered around him, Paul rose up. God is so good. He gives us each other for support and encouragement. Let the saints God has placed in your life gather around you and help you bear the burdens life has brought your way. Always remember Romans 8:28. God will cause all things to work together for good to those who love Him.

Manna Moment

Do you have a friend you can call when the going gets a little rough? If not, consider joining a small group at your church. Be someone others can count on for support and encouragement.

Day 264: He Satisfies Every Need

"He is the God who made the world and everything in it. Since he is Lord of heaven

and earth, he doesn't live in manmade
temples, and human hands can't serve his
needs – for he has no needs. He himself gives
life and breath to everything, and he satisfies
every need there is.

— Acts 17:24-25 (NLT)

God made the world and everything in it, the
people, the animals, the plants, and the creatures in
the sea. Our minds should be at ease knowing that
He fulfills every need, not some needs, but every
need. Whatever need you have, God will satisfy it.
No matter how many needs you have God will take
care of every one of them.

If God takes care of every need, why do we experience lack in our lives? While God is trying to lead
us in the direction of His ample supply we often get
distracted or caught up in pride and venture off on
our own. When we go away from God, lack is what
we find. Just like the prodigal son, we end up with
nothing.

Manna Moment

What need do you have today? Entreat the Lord.
He satisfies every need.

Day 265: He is Not Far

*From one man he made every nation of men,
that they should inhabit the whole earth; and
he determined the times set for them and the*

*exact places where they should live. God did
this so that men would seek him and perhaps
reach out for him and find him, though he is
not far from each one of us.*

—Acts 17:26-27 (NIV)

God made every nation of men to seek Him,
reach out for Him and find Him. Whether we live on
the East Coast or the West Coast, in the South or in
the North, God determines where we should live. No
matter where you call home, He is not far from you.
Reach out for Him today.

Manna Moment

Take a globe and look at all the countries of the
world. Pray for the people of every nation to seek
God and reach out for Him.

Day 266: All Hope Was Gone

*The next day, as gale force winds continued
to batter the ship, the crew began throwing
the cargo overboard. The following day they
even threw out the ship's equipment and
anything else they could lay their hands on.
The terrible storm raged unabated for many
days, blotting out the sun and the stars, until
at last all hope was gone.*

—Acts 27:18-20 (NLT)

Have you ever lost all hope? It is during times of utter hopelessness and helplessness when things look the bleakest, that our God shows us how great He is.

When the stormy winds of life rage around us, we will sometimes be like those on the ship with the apostle Paul. We will be unable to see any light, just dark clouds and strong, harsh winds. We may experience a loss of things that are valuable to us, personal belongings we thought we needed to make our journey through this life successful. You may experience loss, but, like the apostle Paul, your life will be spared.

Manna Moment

If there is a terrible storm raging in your life, blotting out the sun and the stars? Do not lose hope. Anchor yourself in the Lord.

Day 267: All Can Be Saved

We are made right in God's sight when we trust in Jesus Christ to take away our sins. And we all can be saved in this same way, no matter who we are or what we have done.
　　　　　　　　　—Romans 3:22 (NLT)

We cannot be made right in God's sight when we rely on our own good works to get us there. No matter how much we give to charities or volunteer our time to worthy causes, it will not pay the debt of our sins. Only believing in Jesus Christ and the blood He shed on the cross puts us on the road to righteousness. When we put all of our confidence in Jesus Christ to take away our sins we are made right in the sight of God.

God does not show favoritism (Acts 2:11). Notice that His Word says, *all* can be saved, no matter who we are or what we have done. Praise God! Do not believe the enemy when he beats you up about your past, telling you what you have done is so bad it can never be forgiven. Do not let the devil drown you in guilt. If we confess our sins to Him, God forgives us. There is no sin too big or too bad that the blood of Jesus Christ cannot cover. When Jesus hung on the cross and said, "It is finished!" (John 19:30) the wonder working deed was done. The debt was paid for any sin ever committed or to be committed. God is so good.

Manna Moment

Have you confessed your sins to the Lord? Do you trust in Him for your salvation? If not, do it now.

Day 268: No Condemnation

Therefore, there is now no condemnation for those who are in Christ Jesus, because through Christ Jesus the law of the Spirit of life set me free from the law of sin and death.

—Romans 8:1-2 (NIV)

Do you ever feel condemned for some past sin which you have already confessed? Once confessed, the blood of Jesus washes your sins away and you are found innocent in the eyes of God.

The Holy Spirit convicts our heart of sin. The enemy of our souls leads us down the road of condemnation. He accuses us before the Father night and day.

Whenever Satan throws past sin in your face read the above verse. Jesus Christ sets you free from sin and death by the law of the Spirit of life. Condemnation only serves to beat you down. The law of the Spirit of life lifts you up into fellowship with the heavenly Father.

Manna Moment

Is there some sin that Satan uses to haunt you with guilt? Memorize Romans 8:1-2 and whenever the devil throws your past sin in your face, throw the Word of God at him by reciting Romans 8:1-2 out loud.

Day 269: Abba Father

For you did not receive a spirit that makes you a slave again to fear, but you received the Spirit of sonship. And by him we cry, "Abba, Father." The Spirit himself testifies with our spirit that we are God's children.
—Romans 8:15-16 (NIV)

Not everyone experiences a great relationship with their earthly father. However, our heavenly Father is the best Dad anyone could ever hope to have. Our heavenly "Daddy" is perfect and flawless. When we cry out to Him, He hears us. Abba Father leads us and guides us in the right direction. When we stray away, our heavenly Father shows us the way back to Him. He stands with open arms ready to fellowship with us again. He is there to catch us when we fall. He carries us when we do not have the strength to go on. As a loving Father, He only wants the best for His children. He loves us with an everlasting love.

In Mark 14:36, when Jesus was deeply distressed and troubled in Gethsemane, it was "Abba Father" He called out to. Cry out to your heavenly Father today. He is waiting to hear your voice.

Manna Moment

Is there something about your relationship with your earthly father or lack of relationship with him that hinders you from responding to the love and compassion of your heavenly Father? Entreat God to help you forgive your earthly father for all his shortcomings. Open your heart to God and receive from Him what you did not get from your human father.

Day 270: Not Worth Comparing

I consider that our present sufferings are not worth comparing with the glory that will be revealed in us.
—Romans 8:18 (NIV)

What are your present sufferings? Is it frustration, disappointment, anger, depression, weariness, betrayal, loneliness, sickness or financial difficulties? The trials you face in this life are not worth comparing to the glory that will be revealed in you as a child of God.

Whether you are standing in the midst of the fiery furnace or battling a raging storm, comfort yourself with the words of the Apostle Paul in Romans 8:18 and think about the glorious future we have in store for us, to spend eternity in the presence of Almighty God, our Heavenly Father. Our human minds cannot conceive what Almighty God has in store for us, but we do know that it will not be worth comparing to anything we go through in this life. Hallelujah!

Manna Moment

Visualize the most glorious future you can imagine. What does it look like? What does it smell like? What kinds of sounds do you hear? Know in your heart that the future God has for you is considerably better than anything you can imagine or think.

Day 271: He Is Working for Your Good

And we know that God causes everything to work together for the good of those who love God and are called according to his purpose for them.

—Romans 8:28 (NLT)

Whatever happens in your life, no mater how unpleasant or devastating, God will work it all together for good. God will take every heartache, disappointment and loss and use it to bring about something good. When you are mistreated and betrayed by those you trust the most, God is still working all things toward good in your life. Psalm 145:9 tells us, the LORD is good to all.

Manna Moment

Take a moment to meditate on the goodness of God in your life.

Day 272: The Love of God

For I am convinced that neither death nor life, neither angels nor demons, neither the present nor the future, nor any powers, neither height nor depth, nor anything else in all creation, will be able to separate us from the love of God that is in Christ Jesus our Lord.

—Romans 8:38-39 (NIV)

If you are not feeling loved by God stop believing the lies the devil is feeding you. God does love you (insert your name). We should wake up every morning totally overjoyed and absolutely delighted about the fact that God, the very Creator of the universe, loves us. What more could we want than the Father's love? He is the One who orchestrates the whole show; the Master architect with the master plan, the One who has the power over death and sin, the One who gives us eternal life. He is the One who is working on your behalf to give you a future and a hope.

Nothing you have done can separate you from the love of God. The angels in heaven cannot stop God from loving you. Whatever failures you experienced are not enough to stop God from loving you. Jesus loved you enough to give up His life for you on the cross. If you were the only person on this earth, He would have done it just for you. Praise the Lord!

Manna Moment

Do you feel separated from God's love? Meditate on His Word which says nothing can separate you from His love. Believe His Word more than you believe your feelings.

Day 273: Richly Blessed

For there is no difference between Jew and Gentile - the same Lord is Lord of all and richly blesses all who call on him, for,

"Everyone who calls on the name of the Lord will be saved."
> —Romans 10:12-13 (NIV)

Jesus Christ is the Lord of all and He richly blesses all who call on His name. Our Lord is not prejudice and He has no favorites. He loves each and every one of us and He saves every person who calls on His name with a sincere heart. He rescues our souls from hell and He delivers us out of our troubles. He shows us His goodness in the land of the living.

Call on the Lord and be richly blessed in this life and in the one to come.

Manna Moment

What does "richly blessed" mean to you? Describe it. I guarantee that whatever you come up with, God has something a lot better in store for you.

Day 274: Living Sacrifices

Therefore, I urge you, brothers, in view of God's mercy, to offer your bodies as living sacrifices, holy and pleasing to God—this is your spiritual act of worship.
> —Romans 12:1 (NIV)

Our spiritual act of worship is to offer our bodies to God as living sacrifices. As we begin each new day we should dedicate our bodies to Him with the attitude that we are here to be used by Him according to His will and purpose. Let us stop trying to do our own thing and rest on the altar of God. When we present ourselves to Him, may we relinquish control of each member of our bodies: our feet, our hands, our arms, our eyes, our mouths, our minds and our hearts.

On God's altar, we reveal our deepest, most intimate secrets to Him. There is nothing hidden. And we follow Him no matter what our present circumstances look like, because we trust Him with every aspect of our lives. Jesus willingly gave His all for us on the cross. So, offer your body to Him, today, as a living sacrifice, holy and pleasing to its Creator.

Manna Moment

Which part of your body do you have the most difficult time giving over to God? Think of all that Jesus sacrificed for us and give your all to Him.

Day 275: Be Transformed

Do not conform any longer to the pattern of this world, but be transformed by the renewing of your mind. Then you will be able to test and approve what God's will is— his good, pleasing and perfect will.
                                            —Romans 12:2 (NIV)

We are not to follow after the ways of this world. As children of God, He calls us to be different. We are called to be in this world, but not of this world.

303

We are new creatures in Christ and we are to renew our minds according to the Word of God. When we think according to the Word of God, we will be transformed to be more like Jesus. As our minds are renewed, we will walk according to His Spirit and not according to our flesh. Little by little, old ways of thinking are replaced with the knowledge and truth of God. It is a process that eventually encompasses every area of our lives.

When we are transformed, the beauty of the Lord shines through us and attracts others with a desire to know the Lord, Jesus Christ. And we live a life of abundance, peace and joy, in the Lord. Open up His Word, renew your mind and be transformed.

Manna Moment

How do you conform to the ways of this world? Do you get involved with gossip at work? Do you cheat on your taxes? Do you tell "little white lies?" Transform your ways by renewing your mind with the Word of God.

Day 276: The Only Continual Debt

Let no debt remain outstanding, except the continuing debt to love one another, for he who loves his fellowman has fulfilled the law.

—Romans 13:8 (NIV)

This is an appeal to live a debt-free life as well as to fulfill the law of love. The two greatest commandments instruct us to love God and to love our neighbors. Loving one another is a continuous process, not a one time act. To continually love one another requires us to give of ourselves, our time and our resources. It requires us to exercise patience with those who we have difficulty interacting with.

In 1 Corinthians 13:13, the apostle Paul says that love is the greatest. When all is said and done, people will remember how you loved them. May we fulfill the law of love each day of our lives.

Manna Moment

Think of how refreshing it was when someone reached out to you at a time when you needed it most. Reach out to someone with your love today with a phone call, an e-mail or a visit.

Day 277: Overflow with Hope

So I pray that God, who gives you hope, will keep you happy and full of peace as you believe in him. May you overflow with hope through the power of the Holy Spirit.
—Romans 15:13 (NLT)

Hope gives us the promise of a better future. Jeremiah 29:11 tells us God has plans for us to give us hope and a future. Whenever it seems your situation is hopeless, do not believe the lies of your

enemy. The devil wants God's people living discouraged and defeated lives. Keep hope alive! Put your
hope in God and you will not be disappointed. His
plans for you are more glorious and wonderful than
you could ever think or imagine. May your heart and
mind overflow with hope today.

Manna Moment

What are you hoping for? Thank God for the
hope you have within you. Ask Him to keep hope
alive and vibrant within you.

278: Join Me in My Struggle

*I urge you, brothers, by our Lord Jesus Christ
and by the love of the Spirit, to join me in my
struggle by praying to God for me.*
—Romans 15:30 (NIV)

This is a marvelous thing that God has done
for us. Not only do we have God by our side, but
we also have brothers and sisters who can join us
in our struggle as they lift us up in prayer. We all
have conflicts. We enter life with a struggle, wrestling to get out and be free. As we go through life
we encounter many hardships, and we share many
of the same trials. When you are struggling, ask a
fellow believer to join you, by praying for you with
the love of the Holy Spirit within them. On the other
hand, when you see a sister or brother in the midst of

hard times, join her or him by offering up a prayer for their deliverance.

Manna Moment

If you are experiencing a challenging ordeal today, I join you in that grueling struggle by offering up a prayer full of the love of the Spirit. "Dear Heavenly Father, I lift up my dear sisters and brothers who are in the midst of trials and tribulations. May You give them strength and show them the appropriate course of action to be taken. May You keep their hearts and their minds at peace, as they trust in You to show them the way. And may You fill their hearts with joy as You bring about victory in their lives. In the name of Jesus Christ, I pray. Amen."

Day 279: Build on the Foundation

For no one can lay any foundation other than
the one already laid, which is Jesus Christ.
— 1 Corinthians 3:11 (NIV)

Jesus Christ is the foundation on which we must build our lives, in order to withstand the storms of this life. He is the sure foundation. He is stable and dependable. Anything else you choose to build on will crumble and fall when the going gets a little rough.

If you build on human ability and strength what you have built will not withstand the storms. We exist because of our wonderful Creator. And we live, move and have our being in Him. He is the only real foundation. Everything else is temporary. We need to build our lives according to His will and His purpose.

Manna Moment

Are you building your life on the foundation of Jesus Christ? Give it to Him and He will rebuild.

Day 280: Run Your Race

Do you not know that those who run in a race all run, but one receives the prize? Run in such a way that you may obtain it. And everyone who competes for the prize is temperate in all things. Now they do it to obtain a perishable crown, but we for an imperishable crown.
— 1 Corinthians 9:24-25 (NKJ)

We all have our race to run. God has given each one of us our own unique course that we must run. We cannot run someone else's race. As much as I want to control the way my teenage daughter runs her race, I cannot. It is in God's hands. What I can control is how I take each step, making sure it is in the direction God is showing me. In the same way, you can only run the race God has set before you. I pray God would show you the way and give you the strength to take each step in faith. Amen.

Manna Moment

Are you running the race God has before you? If you are on the sideline, appeal to God for the strength and direction you need to get back in the race.

Day 281: A Way Out

So, if you think you are standing firm, be careful that you don't fall! No temptation has seized you except what is common to man. And God is faithful; he will not let you be tempted beyond what you can bear. But when you are tempted, he will also provide a way out so that you can stand up under it.
— 1 Corinthians 10:12-13 (NIV)

Whatever temptations you face today are common to the human race. We are not alone in our struggle against sin. As part of the human experience we share similar temptations. Even Jesus was tempted in every way, just as we are (Hebrews 4:15). Yet He was without sin. Remember that God will not allow us to be tempted beyond what we can bear. And He will also provide a way out. Be careful that you don't fall. When you are tempted and you do not see the way out, pray and ask God to show you the way of escape. The writer of Hebrews 2:18 tells us that even Jesus suffered when he was tempted, and he is able to help those who are being tempted now.

If you are tempted to strike back at someone who has let you have it, instead of opening your mouth and saying something you might regret, ask Jesus to show you the way out. When you are tempted to get even with someone who has done you wrong, call on Jesus for help to do what is right. Our God is faithful. Amen.

Manna Moment

During times of temptation, remember to look for the way out. It may be to close your eyes, leave the room, stop associating with people who bring temptation into your life or confess to someone who can hold you accountable.

Day 282: Love Never Fails

Love is patient, love is kind. It does not envy, it does not boast, it is not proud. It is not rude, it is not self-seeking, it is not easily angered, it keeps no record of wrongs. Love does not delight in evil but rejoices with the truth. It always protects, always trusts, always hopes, always perseveres. Love never fails.
— 1 Corinthians 13:4-8 (NIV)

When questioned about which is the greatest commandment, Jesus replied, to love the Lord your God with all your heart and with all your soul and with all your mind and the second greatest is to love your neighbor as yourself (Matthew 22:37-39). So we are called to love in our horizontal relationships with other people and in our vertical relationship with

God. Everything we do is to be done in love. When others are annoyed or irritated with us, we are to be patient and kind, not rude. We are to put the needs of others before seeking to gratify our own needs.

In other words, as followers of our Lord Jesus Christ, we are called to a higher level. We are called to love the way He loves us. His love never fails. When people strike out at us, we are called to respond in love. When we are betrayed we are not to keep a record of the wrongs done to us and repeat the matter to everyone who will listen. According to the apostle Paul in 1 Corinthians 13:2, if we do not have love we are nothing. Love is the call. Will you answer it?

Manna Moment

Have you have failed to show love to others or in your relationship with God? Make a special effort to respond to those God has in your life with His kind of love.

Day 283: Be on Guard

Be on guard. Stand true to what you believe. Be courageous. Be strong. And everything you do must be done with love.
            —1 Corinthians 16:13-14 (NLT)

Be aware that we have an enemy who roams the earth seeking to steal, kill and destroy. If we let our guard down we run the risk of falling for the wiles of the enemy. The next thing we know, we are entangled in his web of deceit and victimized by his lies. In order to identify a counterfeit you must know the real thing. The only way to recognize Satan's lies is to know the truth found in the Word of God.

The Word is living and active and we can use it to protect our hearts and our minds. We must stay on guard at all times. This helps us stand true to our calling in the Lord Jesus Christ. As the apostle Paul did in his letter to the church in Corinth, I encourage you to be on guard, be courageous, be strong and do all things in love.

Manna Moment

Visualize yourself in the uniform of a guard, looking out for your spiritual, physical, mental and emotional well-being. Envision yourself as a sentry, staying alert for any warning signs that pose a threat.

Day 284: The God of All Comfort

Praise be to the God and Father of our Lord Jesus Christ, the Father of compassion and the God of all comfort, who comforts us in all our troubles, so that we can comfort those in any trouble with the comfort we ourselves have received from God.
　　　　　　　　—2 Corinthians 1:3-4 (NIV)

Do you have any troubles today? Go to the Father of compassion and the God of all comfort. He comforts us in all our troubles, not some, but all.

In our times of grief, sadness or sickness, He is there. Whether we are at the end of our rope, hanging on by a string, emotionally drained or physically wiped out, the comfort of our heavenly Father is there for us. We can be reassured knowing that His loving arms are around us giving us the strength and comfort we so desperately need. And there are times in our lives when He picks us up and carries us through certain trials, just like a shepherd picks up his sheep and carries them close to his heart. Our heavenly Father is full of compassion toward us. And He is the God of all comfort.

Manna Moment

Do you know someone who is suffering a trial similar to one you have experienced? Comfort them with the comfort you received from God when you were in that trial.

Day 285: Rely on God

We were crushed and completely over-whelmed, and we thought we would never live through it. In fact, we expected to die. But as a result, we learned not to rely on ourselves, but on God who can raise the dead.
—2 Corinthians 1:8-9 (NLT)

Do the circumstances in your life have you feeling like you have been completely crushed and trampled upon? Are you totally overwhelmed?

Now is the perfect time to be like the Apostle Paul and learn not to rely on yourself. We must learn to rely on God. All power and wisdom are in His hands. Even though we cannot see our way out of the situation, we have to trust God and His power that is able to bring the dead back to life. Be strengthened in your faith and know with all your heart and mind that God will see you through every circumstance, no matter how difficult.

Manna Moment

Do you need to learn how to rely on God in a particular facet of your life? Offer it up to Him in prayer. Ask Him to help you rely on Him in all areas of your life.

Day 286: Always Led into Triumph

Now thanks be to God who always leads us in triumph in Christ, and through us diffuses the fragrance of His knowledge in every place.
  —2 Corinthians 2:14 (NKJ)

God always leads us into victory in Jesus Christ. Praise the Lord! We just have to follow our Lord and Savior, Jesus Christ and we will triumph over our foes and anything else that comes against us. Instead of wandering off on your own, stay in Christ and you will experience success.

Manna Moment

Think about the past victories God has given to you. What battles are you currently engaged in? Follow God and He will lead you into triumph.

Day 287: Being Transformed

And we, who with unveiled faces all reflect the Lord's glory, are being transformed into his likeness with ever-increasing glory, which comes from the Lord, who is the Spirit.
— 2 Corinthians 3:18 (NIV)

All of us reflect the Lord's glory. We were all made in the image of God, and we are continuously being transformed to be increasingly more like Him. God loves us too much to leave us the way we are. As part of this transformation we shift from thinking its all about us to knowing its all about Him. His glory shines through us and increases as we walk with Him. We serve a faithful God. He who began a good work in us will be faithful to complete it.

Manna Moment

In what ways have you become more like Jesus? In what ways are you still being transformed into His likeness?

Day 288: Struck Down but Not Destroyed

We are hard-pressed on every side, yet not crushed; we are perplexed, but not in despair; persecuted, but not forsaken; struck down, but not destroyed...
— 2 Corinthians 4:8-9 (NKJ)

Are the circumstances of your life pressing in on you from every side? Have you been struck down emotionally or physically, by some hardship in your life? Even in difficult times we can give thanks to God because we know, He always leads us in triumph in Christ (2 Corinthians 2:14). It does not say sometimes, but always! Abide in Christ. You may be struck down, but you will not be destroyed. God will pick you up and guide you into victory.

Manna Moment

When life smacks you around and beats you down reflect on the life of the apostle Paul, described in 2 Corinthians 11:25-28. Among many other things, He was beaten with rods, stoned, and shipwrecked. He suffered hunger, thirst and sleepless nights. However, he fought the good fight. He finished the race and He kept the faith.

Day 289: Look Forward to Everlasting Joys

That is why we never give up. Though our bodies are dying, our spirits are being renewed every day. For our present troubles are quite small and won't last very long. Yet they produce for us an immeasurably great glory that will last forever! So we don't look at the trouble we can see right now; rather, we look forward to what we have not yet seen. For the troubles we see will soon be over, but the joys to come will last forever.
> —2 Corinthians 4:16-18 (NLT)

Never give up. Never give in. Do not quit! Be steadfast. When you feel like quitting, remember, the troubles you see right now will soon be over. Keep on persevering because the troubles are temporary. We must look forward to what we have not yet seen. Look beyond the difficulties and see the great glory they produce for eternity. Look ahead to the everlasting joy that will be ours.

Manna Moment

Have a mental picture of what your victory will look like. Visualize your future joys that will last forever.

Day 290: Not by Sight

We live by faith, not by sight.
— 2 Corinthians 5:7 (NIV)

We are to live by faith, not by the things we can see. The writer of Hebrews tells us that faith is being sure of what we hope for and certain of what we do not see. The things we see are temporary. Our heavenly Father, Whom we do not see, is eternal.

When all we see is lack, by faith we must believe God will give us life in abundance. When all we see is sickness and disease, we must believe God is our healer. If we have suffered injustice, we have to stand in faith, certain that God will give us justice. He will make wrongs, right. He will turn the darkness you see into light. He will turn your mourning into rejoicing. We are to live each day by faith, not by sight.

Manna Moment

Are you looking at your current situation with eyes of faith?

Day 291: A New Creation

Therefore, if anyone is in Christ, he is a new creation; the old has gone, the new has come!
— 2 Corinthians 5:17 (NIV)

When we give our lives to the Lord, we become new creatures. The transformation is as astonishing as the caterpillar which goes into its cocoon and comes out as a beautiful butterfly.

When we invite the Lord into our hearts and lives, the Holy Spirit comes and dwells inside of us and we become a new creation. The old body that was full of darkness and sin becomes a new body that enjoys an abundant life, full of light and truth. The sin is washed away by the blood of Jesus. The light of the Lord floods the darkness. The new creation is set free from bondage. Fear becomes faith. The hope of eternal life replaces the fear of death. The old meaningless life becomes a life of hope, purpose and direction.

Manna Moment

Count all the ways you have become a new creation in Christ.

Day 292: External Conflicts and Inner Fears

For when we came into Macedonia, this body of ours had no rest, but we were harassed at every turn – conflicts on the outside, fears within. But God, who comforts the downcast, comforted us by the coming of Titus,
—2 Corinthians 7:5-6 (NIV)

Demands come from every area of our lives: children, spouses, parents, friends, bosses, business associates and other relationships. As a result of the demands, most of us lead such busy lives. It may seem as though our bodies get no rest.

Like the Apostle Paul, we deal with conflicts on the outside and fears within. We experience conflict on the job, in our marriage relationships, with other believers, and with the world. We have fears within—fear of the unknown, fear of failure or fear of success. In addition, there is the underlying dread of not being loved or of being alone. Fears surround us when it comes to stepping out in faith to do what God has put on our hearts to do. At times, we fear if we try to accomplish anything significant it would only end in failure. In the midst of all our demands, conflicts and fears, God comforts us. He comforts the downcast, the lonely and the fearful.

Manna Moment

Examine each area of your life. In what circumstances are you the most fearful? In what areas are you experiencing conflict? Allow God to be your comforter.

Day 293: God Is Able

And God is able to make all grace abound to you, so that in all things at all times, having all that you need, you will abound in every good work.

—2 Corinthians 9:8 (NIV)

The first four words in this passage of Scripture are the most important ones for us to remember. God is able. No matter what we need, no matter who we are and no matter where we are, He is able. He is able to give you all you need to complete the good work He has called you to. God is able to keep pouring His grace into our lives until it overflows.

Manna Moment

Look at God in relation to your problem. Almighty God who made the heavens and the earth is much bigger than any problem we could ever have. God is more than able.

Day 294: Demolish Strongholds

For though we live in the world, we do not wage war as the world does. The weapons we fight with are not the weapons of the world. On the contrary, they have divine power to demolish strongholds. We demolish arguments and every pretension that sets itself up against the knowledge of God, and we take captive every thought to make it obedient to Christ.
—2 Corinthians 10:3-5 (NIV)

God's divine power destroys any and all of the enemy's strongholds in our lives and in our hearts. Strongholds are any of those areas in our lives where the enemy tries to dominate and defeat us. We have to line up every thought we have with our knowledge of God.

This is the knowledge we want to be in agreement with, that He loves us, that nothing can ever separate us from His love, that He is working for our good and the knowledge that He has a plan for our lives that gives us hope and a future. We also have the knowledge that our battles belong to the LORD!

Manna Moment

What thoughts do you have that go against the knowledge of God? Make them obedient to Christ by speaking the Word of God over them.

Day 295: From Weakness to Power

But he said to me, "My grace is sufficient for you, for my power is made perfect in weakness."
—2 Corinthians 12:9 (NIV)

Admit your weaknesses to God and His power will be made perfect in your weakness. In our weakness His power is made perfect: without fault or defect, and complete. When we have fears and doubts, His power brings faith and peace. During times of confusion, His power passes on wisdom and guidance. In our infirmities, His power provides healing and wholeness. In our despair and hopelessness, His power delivers hope and love. When we are tired and weary, His power brings renewal and restoration.

Manna Moment

Pinpoint specific areas where you are weak. Lift them up in prayer and rely on the power of God to be your strength.

Day 296: Examine Yourselves

Examine yourselves to see whether you are in the faith; test yourselves. Do you not realize that Christ Jesus is in you – unless, of course, you fail the test?
— 2 Corinthians 13:5 (NIV)

We have to examine our hearts to see if we are in the faith or if we are doing things with the wrong motives. Ask yourself these questions. Am I attempting to earn something that is freely given, like my salvation? Am I doing things to receive praise from another person or to be noticed by them? Does fear cause me to do things or stop me from doing the right things? Do I pretend to be someone I am not?

Look at the true motivation of your heart for all that you do. May all we do be from a genuine, sincere and faithful heart.

Manna Moment

Look at yourself in the mirror. Notice your physical characteristics. Now take note of your inner characteristics. Are you loving and kind? Are you patient and peaceful? Do you exercise self-control?

Perform a real self examination and make a decision to change what needs to be changed.

Day 297: Aim for Perfection

Finally, brothers, good-bye. Aim for perfection, listen to my appeal, be of one mind, live in peace. And the God of love and peace will be with you.
—2 Corinthians 13:11 (NIV)

In his final greetings to the church of Corinth, the apostle Paul instructs believers to aim for perfection. There will be times when we miss the mark, however, we must make every effort to reach perfection.

Let us aim for perfection in our relationships with others, in our loving and in serving. Strive for excellence in the work God has given you. Put your all into it and you will be the best you can be.

Manna Moment

Choose one area of your life. What can you do to raise the bar and achieve excellence in this area?

Day 298: Live by Faith

"I have been crucified with Christ; and it is no longer I who live, but Christ lives in me; and the life which I now live in the flesh I live

by faith in the Son of God, who loved me, and delivered Himself up for me."
—Galatians 2:20 (NAS)

As followers of Jesus Christ we ought to live our lives by faith in Him. It is not wise to put more faith in our power, our will or in the knowledge we think we possess. All power and all wisdom belong to our God. It is not prudent to put our faith in our spouse and expect them to be our all in all. Only Jesus can always be there for us. He is the one who will never fail us. Only Jesus loved us enough to stretch out His arms and die for us on the cross.

We must not put our faith in our jobs, our children, our looks, or our possessions. We are to put our faith in the Son of God, our Savior, and the Lord Jesus Christ. When we live our lives by faith, we rely on God for all things and we completely trust Him to come through. When we allow Jesus to live in us, His power works through us and the perfect will of God is accomplished in our lives.

Manna Moment

When God's will does not make sense to you do you step out on faith and follow Him? Think of a time when you went against the feelings of your flesh and blindly followed God. Count the blessings and benefits produced by your faith and God's faithfulness.

Day 299: The Only Thing that Counts

For in Christ Jesus neither circumcision nor uncircumcision has any value. The only thing that counts is faith expressing itself through love.

—Galatians 5:6 (NIV)

What really matters in the brief life we have on this earth, is to believe in God, be totally dependent upon Him and to express our faith in Him through love. As you love God and love others as much as you love yourself you are expressing your faith. Love is an action word. It is something you do. It is when we serve others that our love shines through.

When we serve the Lord, our love for Him shines through. We do not know how many days we have left, so make each day count. Let your faith be expressed through love today. In the words of the apostle Paul, it is the only thing that counts.

Manna Moment

What loving act can you do to express your love for someone today? Carry out that action.

Day 300: Fruit of the Spirit

But the fruit of the Spirit is love, joy, peace, patience, kindness, goodness, faithfulness,

gentleness and self-control. Against such things there is no law.
—Galatians 5:22-23 (NIV)

When we are living our lives according to the Spirit, the fruit of the Spirit will be evident in our lives.

We will walk in love with everyone, including our enemies. We will show love to those who hate us. Our hearts will be full of a deep abiding joy—a joy that is not moved by external circumstances. We will experience peace within and we will strive to live in peace with all men and women. We will be patient at all times, whether standing in the slowest moving line at the grocery store or being stuck in traffic for hours. We can be patient and realize that God has us exactly where He wants us at any given moment and there is probably a reason why He has us there. We will exhibit kindness and goodness wherever we go, always looking for a way to be a blessing to others. Our faithfulness will grow day by day as we continue to walk and trust in Him. If we are bearing the fruit of gentleness and self-control, we will not lose it and go off on people when things do not go our way. The Spirit of God lives in us and when we submit to Him we bear the fruit of His Spirit.

Manna Moment

Ask the Lord to help you submit to His Holy Spirit in you and make your life fruitful.

Day 301: Do Not Become Weary

Let us not become weary in doing good, for at the proper time we will reap a harvest if we do not give up.

—Galatians 6:9 (NIV)

Never give up. When the going gets tough, persevere. If you get discouraged and tired think about the glorious future God has prepared for those who endure to the end. When you think you cannot persist in doing good, call on the LORD for help. Whether it involves initiating a good work or stopping a bad habit, God will give you the strength.

If we persist in doing what God has called us to do, we will have a blessed life in the land of the living and an even better after life. Once we have fought the good fight of faith and completed our course we will reap a wonderful harvest that will last forever.

Manna Moment

What do you do to keep your spirit, soul and body refreshed? Maybe you watch the sun rise or set, take relaxing baths, sit on the beach and listen to the waves, stare at the star lit sky. Be sure to take a time of refreshing as needed.

Day 302: God Chose You

Long ago, even before he made the world, God loved us and chose us in Christ to be holy

*and without fault in his eyes. His unchanging
plan has always been to adopt us into his own
family by bringing us to himself through Jesus
Christ. And this gave him great pleasure.*
　　　　　　　　　—Ephesians 1:4-5 (NLT)

God thought of you before He created the world.
Before He put a twinkling star in the expanse of the
sky, He had you on His mind. You are more important to God than any other creeping, crawling, flying
or swimming creature he created after He thought
about you. He made you in His image. He loves you.
And it gave Him great pleasure to bring you into His
family and call you His daughter or His son. You
matter to God. God chose you.

Manna Moment

Thank God for His unchanging plan to adopt you
into His family through the death and resurrection of
Jesus Christ.

Day 303: Rich in Mercy

*But because of his great love for us, God, who
is rich in mercy, made us alive with Christ
even when we were dead in transgressions—
it is by grace you have been saved.*
　　　　　　　　　—Ephesians 2:4-5 (NIV)

God is rich in mercy and full of grace. Because
of His great love for us, He made us alive with Christ

when we were dead in our sins. He gave us the free gift of salvation. He had mercy on us. He did not give us what we deserved; instead He showed us His kindness and gave us eternal life. Because of His magnificent mercy, we are not condemned. We are able to enjoy a life overflowing with peace and love and full of hope. Our God is so good to us.

Manna Moment

Call on the rich mercy of God.

Day 304: Brought Near

Remember that at that time you were separate from Christ, excluded from citizenship in Israel and foreigners to the covenants of the promise, without hope and without God in the world. But now in Christ Jesus you who once were far away have been brought near through the blood of Christ.
—Ephesians 2:12-13 (NIV)

When Jesus shed His blood and died on the cross to pay the price for our sins, He became a bridge that connects us to our heavenly Father. At one time we were in this dark world without hope and without God. Now we are part of God's family and we have a hope that never ends. He is our Abba Father and we are His dearly loved children. We have been brought near to the throne room of God. His Holy Spirit dwells within us and He desires constant fellowship with us.

Our God is not far. He is near and He watches over you. He will not abandon you.

Manna Moment

Draw a picture of a bridge or take a picture of one with a camera. Look at the picture of the bridge often, as a reminder of how Jesus Christ bridges the gap that separated us from the Father.

Day 305: Mighty Inner Strength

When I think of the wisdom and scope of God's plan, I fall to my knees and pray to the Father, the Creator of everything in heaven and on earth. I pray that from his glorious, unlimited resources he will give you mighty inner strength through his Holy Spirit.
—Ephesians 3:14-16 (NLT)

Our heavenly Father has unlimited resources. He has all we need. He gives us inner strength to do what is right in the face of opposition. He provides mighty inner strength to help us withstand life's challenges and fight the battles that come our way. I pray that Almighty God would give you the mighty inner strength you need to accomplish the mission He has for you today.

Manna Moment

Fall to your knees and pray to the Father that He give you mighty inner strength.

Day 306: Be Kind and Compassionate

Get rid of all bitterness, rage and anger, brawling and slander, along with every form of malice. Be kind and compassionate to one another, forgiving each other, just as in Christ God forgave you.
— Ephesians 4:31-32 (NIV)

When we seethe in anger and resentment, it is like releasing poison into our bodies. *The Merriam-Webster Dictionary* defines malice as the desire to cause injury or distress to another. Fury and rage often lead to desires for revenge, but we are to leave that in the hands of God, for it is written: "It is mine to avenge; I will repay," says the Lord (Romans 12:19). Such emotions are excess baggage we do not want to haul around, because they drag us down. Ease your load by letting go of the excess baggage, so you can soar to new heights.

The angry person is not always loud and boisterous. Sometimes the quiet, soft-spoken person has hostility boiling right beneath the surface, just waiting to erupt.

The Apostle Paul instructs us not to let the sun go down while we are still angry. Resolve issues as soon as possible. Do not let another's unwillingness to forgive prevent you from extending forgiveness. If God in all of His wisdom and holiness forgives us, who are we to hold a grudge against another person? If we strive to be like our heavenly Father we must be kind and compassionate and yes, even forgiving.

Manna Moment

If you are having malicious thoughts, think of ways you can bless the other person instead of harming him or her. Then, put it into action. If you are having problems letting go of anger, bitterness or even rage, think about how God has forgiven you of your transgressions. Think about all the ways He shows you kindness and compassion.

Day 307: The Word Washes

...Christ loved the church and gave himself up for her to make her holy, cleansing her by the washing with water through the word, and to present her to himself as a radiant church, without stain or wrinkle or any other blemish, but holy and blameless.
—Ephesians 5:25-27 (NIV)

Jesus washes us with His word. When we happen to stumble and fall and get a little dirty as we journey through life, Jesus picks us up and cleanses us by washing us with the Word. The Word washes away all guilt, shame and resentment. The Word washes away all bitterness, jealousy and anger. Jesus presents each one of us to Himself without stain, blemishes or wrinkles. In Him we are holy and blameless. May we always keep our hearts open to Him and to His Word.

Manna Moment

Take a bath in His Word today. Look up all the scriptures that pertain to a specific challenge you are dealing with. Read them over and over again until His Word begins to permeate your heart and loosen up the dirt and grime.

Day 308: Carried On to Completion

In all my prayers for all of you, I always pray with joy because of your partnership in the gospel from the first day until now, being confident of this, that he who began a good work in you will carry it on to completion until the day of Christ Jesus.
                                    —Philippians 1:4-6 (NIV)

God has begun a good work in each one of us and we can be confident that He will carry it on to completion. When God created the heavens and the earth, He did not rest until the work was complete. Our God is faithful and his love for us will never fail us. His plans for us are wonderful and more than we could ever think, ask or even imagine. One day, we will be all God wants us to be and the good news is that He already sees us in our completed state. Praise the Lord!

Manna Moment

Glance into the future and write a brief description of what you believe your completed state will look like.

Day 309: Shine like Stars

Do everything without complaining or arguing, so that you may become blameless and pure, children of God without fault in a crooked and depraved generation, in which you shine like stars in the universe...
—Philippians 2:14-15 (NIV)

We are to do everything without complaining, murmuring or arguing, including the responsibilities we dislike. Whatever tasks we have on our "To Do List," we are to do them with a joyful spirit, working unto the LORD. Our heavenly Father had all our days written down before one of them came to be. Do not be like the children of Israel and grumble against the LORD and the race He has selected for you to run.

When we put all of our hearts into the work the Father has called us to do, we will be blameless and pure children of God without fault. As the light of our heavenly Father shines through us we will shine like the stars in the universe and our hearts will twinkle with the joy of the LORD.

Manna Moment

Look up at the stars tonight. Take a mental snap-shot of the brightest star you can find. Remember that is how you shine when you do all the LORD has for you to do without complaining, murmuring or arguing.

Day 310: Embrace Him and Be Embraced

Yes, all the things I once thought were so important are gone from my life. Compared to the high privilege of knowing Christ Jesus as my Master, firsthand, everything I once thought I had going for me is insignificant - dog dung. I've dumped it all in the trash so that I could embrace Christ and be embraced by him.
— Philippians 3:7-9 (THE MESSAGE)

Knowing Christ Jesus as our Master must come first in our lives or anything else we do does not matter. Anything that prevents us from being closer to Jesus must be thrown in the trash. He must be first.

When we know Christ Jesus as our Master, our answer to Him is always "Yes," no matter what He tells us to do. When we know Him as Master our pride goes in the trash and we wear humility. When we know Him as Master we become servants like Jesus. We serve others. When we know Jesus, we lay our cares at His feet and we embrace Him and He embraces us. We must get rid of the clutter we carry around in our lives, so our arms are free to embrace Jesus Christ, our Master. May you embrace our Lord today and be embraced by Him.

Manna Moment

Consider all the things you think are so important in your life. Compare them to the privilege of knowing Christ Jesus. Are there things you need to dump in the trashcan so you can embrace Jesus Christ?

Day 311: Press On

Not that I have already attained, or am already perfected; but I press on, that I may lay hold of that for which Christ Jesus has also laid hold of me. Brethren, I do not count myself to have apprehended; but one thing I do, forgetting those things, which are behind, and reaching forward to those things, which are ahead, I press toward the goal for the prize of the upward call of God in Christ Jesus.

—Philippians 3:12-14 (NKJ)

When we let go of the past, we unload baggage . . . heavy, toilsome baggage. Dragging baggage around drains us of valuable energy. When we let go of the past we find it easier to reach forward. It is a step-by-step process, but God is faithful. He began a good work in us and He will complete it.

No matter how hard the road seems, press on! Even if it seems uphill right now, press on. Sooner or later, one way or another, you will make it to the mountaintop. Even if the road is very rocky, your path will eventually be made smooth. God will always provide exactly what you need for the journey. Praise Him!

Manna Moment

When you find if difficult to press on, see if there is something you need to let go of from the past.

Day 312: Don't Worry...Pray

Don't worry about anything; instead, pray about everything. Tell God what you need, and thank him for all he has done. If you do this, you will experience God's peace, which is far more wonderful than the human mind can understand. His peace will guard your hearts and minds as you live in Christ Jesus.
—Philippians 4:6-7 (NLT)

Do not be anxious for anything. Our God is so great and so wonderful, He does not want us worrying about anything. It is not God's will for you to be worrying and full of anxiety. He wants us to pray about everything, no matter how insignificant you may think it is to God. He cares and His ear is always open.

If you tell Him what you need and thank Him for all He has done in your life God's peace will be yours. We have much to be thankful for as we live our lives on this side of heaven. The peace of God is so grand our human minds cannot comprehend the entire scope of it. But we can experience it in our hearts and in our minds. And His peace will guard your heart and mind, like a shield, from all worry, fear and doubt. May the peace of God be with you.

Manna Moment

Make a list of all you have to thank God for. Give thanks to Him for all these things and welcome God's peace into your heart and mind.

Day 313: Learn the Secret

I know how to live on almost nothing or with everything. I have learned the secret of living in every situation, whether it is with a full stomach or empty, with plenty or little. For I can do everything with the help of Christ who gives me the strength I need.
—Philippians 4:12-13 (NLT)

It is advantageous for us to be like the Apostle Paul and learn the secret of living in any kind of situation the Lord allows in our life. The secret he reveals in verse 13 is to arm yourself with the knowledge that you can do everything and anything when you look to the Lord Jesus Christ for help.

More often than not, people will seek the Lord's help when they are living in lack or in scarcity, but in times of plenty and abundance, we want to take charge. Often times we forget to ask for the Lord's help in taking the right course of action with the fruit He has blessed us with. Learn the secret of asking the Lord for help in all situations, good and bad and He will give you the strength you need. Praise the Lord!

Manna Moment

Ask the Lord what you are to learn in the situation you are currently dealing with.

Day 314: Changing Lives Everywhere

This same Good News that came to you is going out all over the world. It is changing lives everywhere, just as it changed yours that very first day you heard and understood the truth about God's great kindness to sinners.
—Colossians 1:6 (NLT)

The Good News that Jesus Christ has released us from bondage to sin and death gives people all over the world hope.

When we accept Jesus Christ, He changes our lives for the better. Those who are sentenced to death and hell, receive the gift of eternal life. He takes in the orphans and they become members of God's family. Those stumbling around in darkness are brought into His glorious light. He shows the way to those who are lost.

Jesus eliminates fear by strengthening our faith. He renews the hope of the discouraged. Jesus fills the depressed and downcast with joy. The unloved and rejected are infused with the everlasting love of Jesus. He gives purpose and meaning to lives that were plagued by confusion.

Manna Moment

How did your life change when you believed the Good News about Jesus Christ?

Day 315: Held Together in Him

For by him all things were created: things in heaven and on earth, visible and invisible, whether thrones, or powers or rulers or authorities; all things were created by him and for him. He is before all things, and in him all things hold together.
                                  —Colossians 1:16-17 (NIV)

Jesus Christ is before all things. He existed with God before everything else began (John 1:1). This is the perfect order of God. Does your life seem a bit out of order or a little chaotic? Maybe you have allowed someone else or something else to take first place in your life. For your life to be in perfect order,

Jesus must occupy the first position in your heart and in your life.

All things are held together in our Lord and Savior, Jesus Christ. He is the reconciler. He holds us to the Father. If you feel like you are falling apart, live your life in Christ and He will hold all things together. If your marriage is coming apart at the seams put it in the hands of Jesus and it will be held together. If there is a rift in relationships with your children, co-workers or parents, let Jesus mend them and hold them together with His love. Whatever separation exists in your life let Jesus bring it back together and hold it together.

Manna Moment

What would you like Jesus to hold together in your life? See yourself leaving that situation or person in the hands of Jesus. Picture His big, strong hands open and ready to receive it.

Day 316: Overflow with Thankfulness

So then, just as you received Christ Jesus as Lord, continue to live in him, rooted and built up in him, strengthened in the faith as you were taught, and overflowing with thankfulness.

—Colossians 2:6-7 (NIV)

May your roots go down deep and grasp the Lord Jesus Christ firmly. Aspire to be built up in Him with stability and strength. As you meditate on the goodness of the Lord, allow your heart to overflow with thankfulness to the Lord, our Savior, for all the wonderful things He has done and is doing in your life. I pray God would strengthen your faith today and that you would take all your concerns to the Him.

Manna Moment

Compose a list of all you have to be thankful for. Share that list with someone today.

Day 317: Things Above

Since, then, you have been raised with Christ, set your hearts on things above, where Christ is seated at the right hand of God. Set your minds on things above, not on earthly things.
—Colossians 3:1-2 (NIV)

We are in this world but not of this world. The things we go through in this world are temporary. The life we live above, with Jesus will be for all eternity. We need to set our hearts and our minds on things above, the eternal things. Nothing we go through on this earth can compare to the glory we will experience when Christ appears. Whatever trials, injustices, and challenges you face today, just remember they are only temporary. We have the promise of a magnificent future.

Manna Moment

Imagine entering heaven with your new, perfect body and seeing Jesus Christ sitting on His throne, full of glory and beauty. The King of kings is adorned in a majestic robe and a radiant crown. He is surrounded by angels who worship Him day and night. Finally, you see the Lord face to face. What a glorious time that will be when you step into eternity with our Lord and Savior.

Day 318: Clothe Yourselves

Therefore, as God's chosen people, holy and dearly loved, clothe yourselves with compassion, kindness, humility, gentleness and patience.

—Colossians 3:12 (NIV)

When you go to your closet to decide what to wear, remember to put on the garments of compassion, kindness, humility, gentleness and patience.

As God's chosen people we are to put on compassion, a genuine understanding and caring for others. We are to be clothed in humility, not thinking that we are better than anyone else. God created everyone and He loves us all. We are to show kindness and gentleness to each person the Lord brings our way. Our kind deeds speak louder than the outfit we have on. We are to wear patience. God has a designated time for each event under the sun and all things happen according to His timetable.

As we clothe ourselves with these sparkling qualities, we will be more like Jesus Christ, our Savior and our outer garments will be dim compared to His light, shining through us. Amen!

Manna Moment

Write Colossians 3:12 on an index card and hang it in your clothes closet. Read it as a daily reminder to put on compassion, kindness, humility, gentleness and patience.

Day 319: Let Peace Rule

Let the peace of Christ rule in your hearts, since as members of one body you were called to peace. And be thankful.
> —Colossians 3:15 (NIV)

Jesus is the Prince of Peace. He made peace for us with God and He calls us to be at peace with each other. He gives us the peace which surpasses all understanding. Proverbs 14:30 tells us that a heart at peace gives life to the body. Let the peace of Christ rule in your heart.

Manna Moment

Are you involved in a dispute with another person? First, seek God's direction, then contact the other person and do what you can to make peace.

Day 320: Endurance Inspired by Hope

*We continually remember before our God
and Father your work produced by faith, your
labor prompted by love, and your endurance
inspired by hope in our Lord Jesus Christ.*
                    —1 Thessalonians 1:3 (NIV)

Endurance is inspired by hope in our Lord Jesus
Christ. We have to anchor our hope in the Lord and
we will have the stability to withstand the storms
of life. He is alive and He reigns forever and ever.
In Him we have the victory! As long as our hope
is in Him, we can endure the hardships of this life,
knowing that we will sail through the storms and
bright sunny days are coming.

Manna Moment

What hardships has God called you to endure in
this life? Let the hope you have in Jesus inspire you
to endure to the very end.

Day 321: Live to Please God

*On the contrary, we speak as men approved
by God to be entrusted with the gospel. We
are not trying to please men but God, who
tests our hearts.*
                    —1 Thessalonians 2:4 (NIV)

Like the Apostle Paul, we are to live our lives with the desire to please God and not man. Sometimes, the things God calls us to carry out will not be the popular thing to do, from man's perspective. Those who are in our lives may try to discourage us from doing what God wants us to achieve. It is not always easy to step out of the boat and walk on the water with Jesus, but in the end, the benefits are so much greater. Just keep your eyes on Him and do not get distracted by what men are saying.

Those who live to please man will find disappointment, frustration and loneliness. The praise of man is often short lived, shallow and meaningless. When we live to please God we store up our treasures in heaven.

Manna Moment

Has God made you passionate to accomplish something that people around you are advising you against? Take that step of faith and launch God's plan for your life.

Day 322: Caught Up Together

For the Lord himself will come down from heaven, with a loud command, with the voice of the archangel and with the trumpet call of God, and the dead in Christ will rise first. After that, we who are still alive and are left will be caught up together with them in the clouds to meet the Lord in the air. And so

347

we will be with the Lord forever. Therefore, encourage each other with these words.
— 1 Thessalonians 4:16-18 (NIV)

I encourage you with these words, which Apostle Paul wrote to the believers in Thessolonica. You may be wondering why these words are so encouraging.

First of all, it is incredibly exciting to think about the long-awaited day when our Lord and Savior, Jesus Christ, will come down from heaven and make His grand appearance. Secondly, Jesus is coming back and furthermore we will have the extra-added benefit of joining Him in the air. The third aspect of this wonderful plan God designed for us is the best part of the whole spectacular picture. We will dwell with the Lord, forever and ever.

Oh, how that blesses my heart, because that means we can look at whatever trials, temptations, or disappointments going on in our lives right now and put them in proper perspective. They are temporary. Yet, our time with Jesus is eternal. Whatever happens on this side of heaven does not compare to the glorious days we will spend in the presence of our Lord and Savior, Jesus Christ.

As long as we look at the end result, we will be better equipped emotionally to deal with what is going on today. As if this were not enough, the fourth benefit to God's awesome plan is that we will be reunited with loved ones who have passed on before us. God is so good! What an absolutely marvelous promise for those of us who are in Christ.

Manna Moment

When you need a little encouragement, look up at the sky and imagine being caught up in the clouds to meet the Lord and be with Him forever.

Day 323: Joy, Prayer and Thankfulness

Be joyful always; pray continually; give thanks in all circumstances, for this is God's will for you in Christ Jesus.
— 1 Thessalonians 5:16-18 (NIV)

Be filled with the joy of the LORD, the joy that comes from knowing Him. James even tells us to consider it all joy when we face trials of many kinds (James 1:2). The joy of the LORD is your strength.

Pray at all times. Cry out to God in times of doubt, confusion, anxiety or fear. Call upon God during times of great disappointment, failure or conflict. Even in times of peace, and total exhilaration take time to pray. The ear of the LORD is always open. He does not sleep and He does not slumber.

Give thanks in all circumstances, according to the will of God. No matter how desperate your current state of affairs, there is always something to be thankful for.

Manna Moment

What fills your heart with joy? What do you need to lift up in prayer continually? Give thanks to God, no matter what the circumstance of your life.

Day 324: The LORD Is Faithful

But the Lord is faithful, and he will strengthen and protect you from the evil one.
—2 Thessalonians 3:3 (NIV)

The LORD is faithful. You can count on Him to be there when you need Him. He is always there for us. Jesus is the friend who sticks closer than a brother. He provides for all of our needs. He is the Great Physician. He heals our physical and emotional wounds. He is our sure foundation, the rock on which we stand. The LORD gives us strength and protects us from the evil one.

Manna Moment

Tell someone how God has shown you His faithfulness.

Day 325: Deeper Understanding

May the Lord bring you into an ever deeper understanding of the love of God and the endurance that comes from Christ.
—2 Thessalonians 3:5 (NLT)

If we could only understand how much God really loves us, we would truly be set free and totally healed emotionally. His love for us is so deep; He formed us when we were in our mother's wombs. His love for us is unconditional, which means that whatever we do, He will not love us any less. And there is nothing we can do to make Him love us more, that sets us free from doing works in an attempt to get Him to love us more.

God sent His only Son, Jesus to the earth in a human body because He loved us and wanted to reconcile us back into fellowship with Him. It was love that held Jesus to the cross, to pay the price for our sins. Do not take fellowship with God for granted. It is an awesome privilege we have to be able to fellowship with God, our Heavenly Father and Jesus Christ, our Savior. Nothing will ever separate us from the love of God. May your understanding of God's love grow deeper each day.

Manna Moment

How has God revealed His love to you?

326: Peace at All Times

Now may the Lord of peace himself give you peace at all times and in every way. The Lord be with all of you.
                    —2 Thessalonians 3:16 (NIV)

I pray you would find peace in whatever set of circumstances you face today. Whether it is on the job, in the home or in a personal relationship, the Lord gives you peace at all times and in every situation. When you feel like you are being bombarded from all sides, reach out and hold onto the peace that our Lord Jesus Christ gives. Amen.

Manna Moment

Do you experience the peace of God at all times? When you feel your peace ebbing away, shift your focus away from the problem and onto the peace maker, Jesus Christ.

Day 327: Outpouring of Grace, Faith and Love

The grace of our Lord was poured out on me abundantly, along with the faith and love that are in Christ Jesus.

—1 Timothy 1:14 (NIV)

May the Lord completely fill us with His grace, faith and love. As the grace of the Lord is poured on us in abundance we become personally acquainted with the unmerited favor of God. Our sins are forgiven and we are no longer bound to the mistakes of the past.

After we have been showered with the faith that is in Christ Jesus, we live by that faith and not by our sight. If the world tells us "we cannot", our great faith tells us "we can and we will," because we know all things are possible with God.

When our souls are flooded with the love of Christ Jesus, we walk in unconditional love, forgiving everyone, just as He forgave us. Let the grace, faith and love of our Lord Jesus Christ work together in us to influence the world for the Him.

Manna Moment

How has God poured out His grace, love and faith on you? Think of ways you can make use of what you have received to inspire others to pursue grace, faith and love.

Day 328: The Unseen One

Glory and honor to God forever and ever. He is the eternal King, the unseen one who never dies; He alone is God. Amen.
          —1 Timothy 1:17 (NLT)

Give glory and honor to God. Acknowledge that He alone is God. He is the only true and living God. He will never die. All power and authority belong to God. The world and all that is in it, belongs to the LORD (Psalm 50:12).

Even though we cannot see Him we believe in Him, that is faith. Faith believes that which it cannot see or understand. May your faith in God be strengthened today.

Manna Moment

When did you become aware of the reality of our unseen, eternal King?

Day 329: Have You Been Shipwrecked?

Timothy, my son, I give you this instruction in keeping with the prophecies once made about you, so that by following them you may fight the good fight, holding on to faith and a good conscience. Some have rejected these and so have shipwrecked their faith.
— 1 Timothy 1:18-19 (NIV)

Are you at risk of being shipwrecked in your faith? Have the raging winds of life turned your boat over? Did the violent waves of adversity upset the smooth course you started out on? If so, get in your lifeboat with Jesus and continue to hold on to your faith.

Without faith you will drown in a sea of doubt and defeat. Listen to the words of the apostle Paul when he was in a ship and caught up in the midst of a violent, raging storm for many days. He urged his traveling companions to keep up their courage (Acts 27:22).

Manna Moment

Here are some ways you can hold on to faith and a good conscience when you are at risk of suffering shipwreck: Memorize and recite Scriptures that build your faith. Fast and pray throughout the storm. Seek God's will for the situation. Do what you know to be the right things and maintain a good conscience. What other ways can you think of to fight a good fight of faith?

Day 330: At the Right Time

For at the right time Christ will be revealed from heaven by the blessed and only almighty God, the King of kings and Lord of lords.
— 1 Timothy 6:15 (NLT)

King Solomon tells us in Chapter 3 of Ecclesiastes that there is a time for everything. There is an appointed time when our Lord and Savior, Jesus Christ will be revealed to the world in all of His glory and splendor. All those who know Him, look forward to this day.

However, now is the time to worship Him in spirit and in truth. Thank Almighty God for sending His only Son down to earth that first Christmas day, to save us. Hallelujah!

Manna Moment

Are you waiting for the right time for something the Lord has spoken to become a reality in your life? Stand in prayer and faith and at the right time it will manifest in your life.

Day 331: Power, Love and Self-discipline

For God has not given us a spirit of fear and timidity, but of power, love, and self-discipline.

—2 Timothy 1:7 (NLT)

God has given us a spirit of power to be over-comers. His power working through us helps us to be victorious, to rise above the circumstances that try to crush us.

God has given us a spirit of love so that we may love our neighbors as much as we love ourselves. His Word instructs believers to love other believers. He desires for us to love our enemies. He wants husbands to love their wives and children to love their parents. Above all, we should love the LORD our God with all our hearts, minds, souls and strength.

He has given us a spirit of self-discipline so we may do what is right, in spite of how we feel or what others tell us. We have a spirit of self-discipline so we can live self-controlled, upright and godly lives, which bring glory and honor to God. May you be filled with the Spirit of the Lord and walk in His power, love and self-discipline.

Manna Moment

What fears do you have? What situations cause you to lose courage and weaken your self-confidence? Ask God to replace the fear and timidity in you with His power, love and self-discipline.

Day 332: Fight the Good Fight

I have fought the good fight, I have finished the race, I have kept the faith. Now there is in store for me the crown of righteousness, which the Lord, the righteous Judge, will award to me on that day—and not only to me, but also to all who have longed for his appearing.

—2 Timothy 4:7-8 (NIV)

Fight the good fight of faith. Fight your battles in the name of the Lord. Like David, we all have our giants to contend with. We are confronted with challenges. Mountains rise up and block our paths. But our God is greater. Praise the LORD!

Remember, our struggle is not against flesh and blood, but against rulers, authorities and powers of this dark world and against the spiritual forces of evil in the heavenly realms (Ephesians 6:12). Through it all, hold tightly, onto your faith and receive the crown of righteousness that is waiting for you.

Manna Moment

Take note of what tools and resources you have to help you fight the good fight of faith. Here are just a few: His Holy Spirit within you, His Word, prayer, fasting, wise counsel from mature Christians, fellowship, praise and worship.

Day 333: He Stands With You

The first time I was brought before the judge, no one was with me. Everyone had abandoned me. I hope it will not be counted against them. But the Lord stood with me and gave me strength...
                              —2 Timothy 4:16-17 (NLT)

At the most difficult times in our lives we may be abandoned by all. However, the Lord always stands with us. He is our source of infinite strength. If we are to be victorious we must learn how to rely on Him alone, in every circumstance. When you are going through trials, remember that the Lord stands with you and He gives you strength.

Manna Moment

Write, "He stands with me." on a sticky and put it in a place where you will look at it two or three times a day, maybe your calendar, appointment book, hand-held organizer, mirror, or refrigerator.

Day 334: Because of His Mercy

But when the kindness and love of God our Savior appeared, he saved us, not because of righteous things we had done, but because of his mercy. He saved us through the washing of rebirth and renewal by the Holy Spirit,
                              —Titus 3:4-6 (NIV)

We are saved because God had mercy on us. We did not receive salvation based on any good works we carried out. Salvation shows us God's kindness and His never-ending love because He removed the pressure on us to perform. We are not pressured or driven to accomplish a list of demands in order to receive salvation. All we have to do is open our hearts and receive the free gift of eternal life by accepting Jesus Christ as our Savior. God takes care of the rest.

This free gift is in stark opposition to the ways of the world. Throughout our lives people require us to perform. During our school years, parents and teachers expect us to get good grades and some children are sentenced with strict punishment when they fail to fulfill the expectations of their parents. Sometimes we are ridiculed, shunned and even rejected if our performance does not exceed the expectations of those around us. On our jobs we are evaluated on the basis of how well we perform. Employees receive performance ratings which may even determine if they remain in their positions. Professional athletes, entertainers, and people like that, have to perform for their contract to be renewed.

Praise God that He saves us from sin and death because of His mercy. When we receive Jesus Christ as our Savior, He washes away our sins and gives us a new life. Thank God for His marvelous, magnificent mercy!

Manna Moment

Describe to someone how it feels to be a beneficiary of God's mercy.

Day 335: Gain a Full Understanding

I always thank my God as I remember you in my prayers, because I hear about your faith in the Lord Jesus and your love for all the saints. I pray that you may be active in sharing your faith, so that you will have a full understanding of every good thing we have in Christ.

—Philemon 4-6 (NIV)

The Apostle Paul is writing to Philemon, a dear friend and fellow worker, someone he consistently prayed for. Paul's prayer for Philemon was for him to actively share his faith. As we actively share our faith with others we gain a full understanding of every good thing we have in our Lord and Savior, Jesus Christ. God has not called everyone to stand in the pulpit to preach, but He does bring people into our lives, if only for a brief moment, who He wants us to share our faith with. Just by telling others what God has done in our lives we may encourage them and change their lives forever.

How can they believe if they do not hear the great things the Lord does for His people? We all have a story to tell and as we share our story, our faith shines through to others and our eyes see more clearly all the good things we have in the Lord. As often as the opportunity presents itself, share your faith so others may hear about your faith in the Lord and your love for all the saints. Then you will gain a full, deeper understanding of every good thing we have in Christ.

Manna Moment

Share your story about what God has done in your life with someone today.

Day 336: Enter into Rest

There remains therefore a rest for the people of God. For he who has entered His rest has himself also ceased form his works as God did from His. Let us therefore be diligent to enter that rest...
—Hebrews 4:9-11 (NKJ)

May we all enter into the rest God has for us. Slip into the rest that comes when we trust in the Lord with all our heart, mind and soul. When we stop trying to force our own will and yield to the will of God we become acquainted with His rest. It is a quiet peaceful rest that comes when we give it all to God. Amen.

Manna Moment

Close your eyes and imagine yourself resting in the arms of our Lord. Open your ears and listen to the voice of Abba Father saying, "Rest, My child. Enter into My rest."

Day 337: He Sympathizes with Our Weaknesses

For we do not have a high priest who is unable to sympathize with our weaknesses, but we have one who has been tempted in every way, just as we are – yet was without sin. Let us then approach the throne of grace with confidence, so that we may receive mercy and find grace to help us in our time of need.
—Hebrews 4:15-16 (NIV)

We have a High Priest who can sympathize with our weaknesses. He knows the trials we face. Therefore, we can feel comfortable when we approach His throne of grace. We can be confident that He understands the road on which we walk. At His throne, we find help in our time of need and God pours His grace upon us.

Manna Moment

Approach the throne of grace and receive God's mercy. Thank our Lord Jesus Christ for sympathizing with our weaknesses and providing help in our time of need.

Day 338: Faith and Patience

We do not want you to become lazy, but to imitate those who through faith and patience inherit what has been promised.
—Hebrews 6:12 (NIV)

It is through faith and patience that we inherit the promises of God. Faith involves a complete trust in God, a believing without seeing, a deep peace and total dependence on Him. And when we have patience we calmly wait on the Lord without complaining, getting anxious, giving up or giving in. May God give us the faith and patience to stand on His promises so we can receive all He has for us.

Manna Moment:

Think of a desire God fulfilled after you waited patiently and stood in faith. Let that success be the catalyst for continual and complete reliance on God.

Day 339: Draw Near

...let us draw near to God with a sincere heart in full assurance of faith, having our hearts sprinkled to cleanse us from a guilty conscience and having our bodies washed with pure water.
—Hebrews 10:22 (NIV)

Draw near to God each day by spending time sitting at His feet, like Mary. Listen for His still small voice. He is a mighty, awesome God. Enjoy just being in His Presence. In His Presence there is fullness of joy. Do not be like Jonah and run away from the LORD, but instead draw near. The safest place to be is by His side. Don't delay. Come just as you are.

Manna Moment

How many ways can you draw near to the God? Here are just a few: sing Him a song, write a poem for Him, talk to Him, listen to Him, read His Word, play a musical instrument or tell Him all the things you are grateful for.

Day 340: Persevere and Receive

You need to persevere so that when you have done the will of God, you will receive what he has promised.
—Hebrews 10:36 (NIV)

Patiently endure the trials and temptations that come your way, without a grumble or complaint. After you have been obedient you will receive what God has promised. The words He speaks come to pass. His faithfulness extends to all generations.

Among His promises are peace, love, joy and eternal life. He promises that if we search for Him with all of our heart we will find Him. His Word promises that no weapon formed against a servant of the LORD will prosper. If we delight ourselves in the LORD, He promises to give us the desires of our heart. His Word is full of wonderful promises which we will receive with perseverance.

Manna Moment

What promises are you standing on? Write them down and review them at least twice a day.

Day 341: Impossible to Please God without Faith

So, you see, it is impossible to please God without faith. Anyone who wants to come to him must believe that there is a God and that he rewards those who sincerely seek him.
—Hebrews 11:6 (NLT)

First of all we must believe there is a God. God has given to each one of us a measure of faith. We have to take the faith we have and water it with the Word. As we live our lives and get to know the faithfulness of God our faith grows stronger.

Then we must believe that God rewards those who sincerely seek Him. Sincere seeking comes from the heart. It is not just going through the motions, but it is a longing in the heart that cries out for more of Him.

When we find Him we have to believe He wants to reward us. Do you believe that God wants to reward you? So often we feel all we deserve is punishment for some wrong we have done. We must believe our heavenly Father wants to reward His children like any loving parent.

Manna Moment

Think about the person who had the most positive influence on your life. List all the ways God is even more concerned about your total well-being.

Day 342: Fix Our Eyes Upon Him

Therefore, since we are surrounded by such a great cloud of witnesses, let us throw off everything that hinders and the sin that so easily entangles, and let us run with perseverance the race marked out for us. Let us fix our eyes on Jesus, the author and perfecter of our faith...

—Hebrews 12:1-2 (NIV)

Each one of us has been given a race to run. If there is anything hindering us from running our race with perseverance, let us throw it off. We do not need to hold onto anything that will cause us to fall or be distracted from completing our course. As you run, keep your eyes on the goal, the Lord Jesus Christ. Instead of fixing your eyes on your problems, fix them on Jesus Christ and Him alone and you will reach the finish line. Amen.

Manna Moment

Is there anything hindering you from running the race marked out for you? What do you need to throw off?

Day 343: Pure Joy!

Consider it pure joy, my brothers, whenever you face trials of many kinds, because you know that the testing of your faith develops perseverance. Perseverance must finish its work so that you may be mature and complete, not lacking anything.
—James 1:2-4 (NIV)

Are you facing trials of many kinds? Think about it as a joyful thing that is happening to you. As your faith is tested, perseverance and endurance are developed within your character and that brings about maturity. You will be complete and not lack anything. In order to do this we must keep our perspective on the end result as we go through different kinds of difficulties, knowing that God will bring us through. And in the end, we will not lack anything. We will have more than we need.

Manna Moment

How can you keep your joy in the midst of trials? When your joy starts seeping out, visualize the perfect end result of the trial. Then, thank God for developing perseverance and maturity in you.

Day 344: Lacking Wisdom

If any of you lacks wisdom, he should ask God, who gives generously to all without finding fault, and it will be given to him. But when he asks, he must believe and not doubt, because he who doubts is like a wave of the sea, blown and tossed by the wind.
— James 1:5-6 (NIV)

As you travel along on the road of life you will encounter many crossroads, where you must decide which way to go. There will be obstacles you need to get over, crawl under, go around or wait for God to remove. Only God knows the best way to go and the most advantageous time.

To reach our God given destination we must ask Him for the wisdom we need to go in the right direction. The Word tells us He will not find fault, but He will give wisdom to us. The only condition is that we must believe when we ask. Believe that He is able and that He will do it. Let there be no doubting. Ask God to remove any doubt and unbelief.

There will be times when the way He directs us to go will not seem like the easier way, but we have to sincerely believe that our God knows what is best. He wrote the Book and He sees the big picture. He is the only one who knows how it will all come together.

Manna Moment

Are you in the middle of a trial right now? What doubts do you have regarding the situation? Ask God to remove your doubts and strengthen your faith.

Day 345: Every Good and Perfect Gift

Every good and perfect gift is from above, coming down from the Father of the heavenly lights, who does not change like shifting shadows.

—James 1:17 (NIV)

Think about all the good and perfect gifts you have received in your life. Each and every one of them has come down to us from our heavenly Father, who created the heavenly lights. He is a gracious Father who likes to give good gifts to His children, such as love, peace, joy, safety, freedom, comfort, family and friends. The most important gift He gives is the gift of eternal life. As we reflect on the goodness of the LORD, we see His blessings in every aspect of our lives.

Manna Moment

What do you consider God's most perfect gift to you? Thank Him for it.

Day 346: Come Near

Submit yourselves, then, to God. Resist the devil, and he will flee from you. Come near to God and he will come near to you.
— James 4:7-8 (NIV)

Submit to God. Let go of your ways and yield to God's way. His way is always the better way. Surrender all to Him, your plans, your thoughts, your feelings, your wishes and your desires. Acknowledge that the LORD is in control of your life.

As you draw near to God, He will draw near to you. When you get alone to spend time with Almighty God, you are drawing near to Him. The access to God is wide open at all times. In Genesis 3:8-9, the LORD God walked in the garden in the cool of the day, and He called to Adam. He wants to fellowship with you like He did with Adam and Eve. Today, He calls *your* name. As you converse with the LORD, imagine both of you walking in the garden of paradise in the cool of the day. What a pleasant thought!

Manna Moment

Recall a time when you felt extremely close to God. How can you maintain that closeness?

Day 347: Humble Yourselves Before the Lord

Humble yourselves before the Lord, and he will lift you up.

—James 4:10 (NIV)

When we humble ourselves before the Lord, we admit to Him and to ourselves, that we cannot do it on our own. We realize we do not know what is best for us and we yield to Him because we trust Him to lead us in the right direction. We bring all of our *stuff* to Him. We turn everything over to Him, the good, the bad and the ugly. We allow Him to use it in our lives according to His will and His purpose. When He says to let something go we let it go instead of trying to justify why we must hold onto it. When He says to forgive someone we forgive them.

When you humble yourself before the Lord, you acknowledge that all of your success is because of Him and you give Him all the glory. In due time, God will lift up those who are humble. He will pick you up out of the dry, dead desert and place you in green pastures, beside quiet waters, where there is life and life more abundantly.

Manna Moment

Are you wrestling with pride or conceit? In a posture of humility confess it to the LORD.

Day 348: Shielded by His Power

Praise be to the God and Father of our Lord Jesus Christ! In his great mercy he has given us new birth into a living hope through the resurrection of Jesus Christ from the dead, and into an inheritance that can never perish, spoil or fade—kept in heaven for you, who through faith are shielded by God's power until the coming of the salvation that is ready to be revealed in the last time.

—1 Peter 1:3-5 (NIV)

God's awesome power is our shield. In His great mercy He protects us and hides us from those who would harm us.

This same power that guards us created heaven and earth and raised Jesus from the dead. God goes before us and His power shields us from the flaming arrows of the evil one. Wise men and women follow closely behind the LORD, so they do not venture out on their own, exposed and vulnerable to the enemy. Make each step you take, a step of faith. Follow closely behind God and through faith, God's power will be your shield.

Manna Moment

Thank God for His invisible yet powerful shield of protection.

Day 349: Do Not Be Surprised

Dear friends, do not be surprised at the painful trial you are suffering, as though something strange were happening to you. But rejoice that you participate in the sufferings of Christ, so that you may be overjoyed when his glory is revealed.

— 1 Peter 4:12-13 (NIV)

Do not be surprised when you go through painful trials. Fiery ordeals are no strange thing. Our Lord and Savior suffered greatly as He was beaten and bruised for us. Jesus bore all of our sins upon His body. He was in agony as He hung on the cross to die for us. In all of our disappointments, setbacks, trials and tribulations remember the affliction of the Lord Jesus Christ. No one knows torment as well as our Lord and Savior. He can relate to all of our suffering. And may we look forward to His glory that is to be revealed and the abundant joy that will be ours.

Manna Moment

What steps do you take when encountering difficult, painful trials? A good first step is to give it to God and then think of all Jesus went through during His life on earth.

Day 350: Humble Yourselves Under His Hand

Humble yourselves, therefore, under God's mighty hand, that he may lift you up in due time. Cast all your anxiety on him because he cares for you. Be self-controlled and alert. Your enemy the devil prowls around like a roaring lion looking for someone to devour. Resist him, standing firm in the faith, because you know that your brothers throughout the world are undergoing the same kind of sufferings.

—1 Peter 5:6-9 (NIV)

First, we must humble ourselves under God's mighty hand and then He will provide the strength we need to stand firm against the devil. The process of humbling ourselves necessitates that we relinquish our way of doing things and embrace God's way. In the course of humbling ourselves, we admit to God that we are helpless and powerless to do anything in our own strength. When we humble ourselves we are under the protective covering of our heavenly Father. He becomes our strength and we are able to stand firm in our faith.

In addition, our heavenly Father invites us to unload all of our anxiety on Him. God cares too much about us to have us weighed down by various burdens. We are unable to raise our hands and give God the praise He deserves if we hold onto our worries and concerns. Make sure that once you have given them to God, you do not pick them up again.

Manna Moment

Hold your right hand out in front of you, face down and fingers together. Now make a fist with your left hand and slide it under you right hand. Let this be a mental picture of what it looks like, spiritually, when you get on your knees and humble yourself under the mighty hand of God. Notice that in this position, God covers us and He is our protection against the attacks of our enemy.

Day 351: God Will Restore You

And the God of all grace, who called you to his eternal glory in Christ, after you have suffered a little while, will himself restore you and make you strong, firm and steadfast. To him be the power for ever and ever. Amen.
— 1 Peter 5:10-11 (NIV)

Whatever suffering we endure, we must remember that suffering is a temporary condition. Each one of us is subject to times of suffering. The extent of the hardship may be a matter of minutes or it could go on for a number of years. The magnitude of the suffering will vary from manageable to unbelievably excruciating. No matter what the duration or intensity, when compared to eternity, all of our suffering is for a little while. After you have suffered for a little while, God will restore you, physically, mentally and spiritually. He will give you strength and make you secure.

Manna Moment

Think about the most intense suffering you have endured. Recall how God brought you through it. List all the ways you were made stronger in that situation. Thank God for being a God of restoration.

Day 352: Everything for Life

His divine power has given us everything we need for life and godliness through our knowledge of him who called us by his own glory and goodness.

—2 Peter 1:3 (NIV)

Are you lacking anything? God has given you everything you need for life. The past tense means it is already done.

His Word tells us He has already given us everything we need for life and godliness. It does not say *some* things or a *few* things, but *everything*. We are to stand in faith and believe God that we have all we need, regardless of the circumstances we see today.

He gives us everything we need for life and godliness *through our knowledge of Him*. If we lack anything, we need to learn more about our heavenly Father and His divine nature. As we spend time with God and become more intimately acquainted with Him, our knowledge of Him increases. According to 2 Peter 1:3, it is through this process of getting to know God that He gives us everything we need to live a godly life. It is His divine power at work within us and our knowledge of Him, who is the truth, which sets us free to receive all that pertains to life and godliness.

When you are ready to receive, reach out and take what you need for life. Just like a gift that is offered, you have to take it if you are going to enjoy its benefits.

Manna Moment

Reflect on all God has given you over the course of your life. Thank Him for it.

Day 353: He Knows How

God rescued Lot out of Sodom because he was a good man who was sick of all the immorality and wickedness around him. Yes, he was a righteous man who was distressed by the wickedness he saw and heard day after day. So you see, the Lord knows how to rescue godly people from their trials...
—2 Peter 2:7-9 (NLT)

Whatever trials or challenges you face today, remember that the Lord knows how to rescue His people from their troubles. Look to Him and call on His name. He knows how to rescue you from all adversity. No ordeal is too difficult for the Lord to handle. Your affliction will not confuse Him or make Him wonder how He is going to handle it. Our God knows how because all wisdom belongs to Him. It is not guesswork with Him. Praise the Lord!

Manna Moment

Are you in the midst of a fiery trial right now? Meditate on the above verse (2 Peter 2:7-9) until you know with every fiber of your being that your heavenly Father knows how to rescue you from your trials.

Day 354: He Is Patient

But do not forget this one thing, dear friends: With the Lord a day is like a thousand years, and a thousand years are like a day. The Lord is not slow in keeping his promise, as some understand slowness. He is patient with you, not wanting anyone to perish, but everyone to come to repentance.
—2 Peter 3:8-9 (NIV)

The Lord's compassion extends to every person He has created. Every person that walks on the face of this earth was created by God. Our heavenly Father breathed the breath of life into each one of us. The blood of Jesus, His Son, covers the sins of the world. He died once and for all to pay the price for the past, present and future sins of each and every person that has ever lived. It is not His desire that anyone should perish.

The Lord works in the lives of unbelievers to bring them to the point of repentance and salvation. He wants everyone to repent of their sins and enter into a relationship with Him. He waits patiently, for us to confess our sins and acknowledge Him as our Lord and Savior. It is comforting to know that He is patient.

Manna Moment

Thank the Lord for His wonderful patience. Pray for your loved ones who are not walking with the Lord right now.

Day 355: Live in the Light

This is the message we have heard from him and declare to you: God is light; in him there is no darkness at all. If we claim to have fellowship with him yet walk in darkness, we lie and do not live by the truth. But if we walk in the light, as he is in the light, we have fellowship with one another, and the blood of Jesus, his Son, purifies us from all sin.
— 1 John 1:5-7 (NIV)

Jesus is the light of the world. When we walk in the light we enjoy wonderful fellowship with Him. If there be any darkness in you, expose it to the light. If there is any deep depression, any burning anger, any ongoing worry or anxiety, any lingering unforgiveness, any burrowing bitterness or any pretentious pride let the light of God chase it away.

God's light is full of joy, love, peace, mercy and humility. As we live in the light, the blood of Jesus cleanses us from all sin. Choose to live in the light of God's presence each and every moment of the day, basking in the radiant light of His glory.

Manna Moment

Look at each area of your life. Are there any areas of darkness? Reveal it to God and ask Him to help you let it go.

Day 356: Do His Will and Live Forever

Do not love the world or anything in the world. If anyone loves the world, the love of the Father is not in him. For everything in the world—the cravings of sinful man, the lust of his eyes and the boasting of what he has and does—comes not from the Father but from the world. The world and its desires pass away, but the man who does the will of God lives forever.

—1 John 2:15-17 (NIV)

Let your love be for God and the people He has created, not for anything in the world. The world and all it has to offer will pass away. It is only here temporarily. It is pointless to brag about what you have on this earth or what you do. First of all, what you have on this earth will disappear like a puff of smoke. It will be as if it never existed. We may as well be like the apostle Paul and count it all as rubbish. It has no value in the eternal scope of things.

Secondly, you can do nothing without God. It is only by His grace and in His strength that we are able to do anything. Those who are in Christ and do the will of God will live forever. Obedience is the key to living forever. Our heavenly Father has given each one of us a purpose. We all have our own specific course to complete and at the end of our journey we all hope to hear the words "Well done, good and faithful servant." Obey the calling God has placed inside of you and enjoy living forever in the presence of the LORD.

Manna Moment

Has God instructed you to do something and you have not quite found the time? I urge you to put the things God has instructed you to do at the top of your list of priorities.

Day 357: Great Is the Love

How great is the love the Father has lavished on us, that we should be called children of God! And that is what we are! The reason the world does not know us is that it did not know him.

—1 John 3:1 (NIV)

The love of the Father is so great that He calls us His children. The love of God is so vast, no matter what we do or where we go all we have to do is call on His name and He is there for us.

When we are drowning in the sea of life it will be His hand that reaches down and pulls us up out of the deep waters. When we are at our breaking point and sure we are about to crumble into a million pieces, He will be the One who holds us together. His love is so great that after we mess up and ask Him to forgive us He doesn't throw our offense back up in our face. He forgives us and welcomes us back into His arms to fellowship with Him. His love for us is so great that His eye is constantly on us and His arms always protecting us.

Manna Moment

Do you feel the awesome love of God? Meditate of the fact that Jesus loves us so much, He gave His very own life as a sacrifice.

Day 358: We are Overcomers

You, dear children, are from God and have overcome them, because the one who is in you is greater than the one who is in the world.
— 1 John 4:4 (NIV)

We are overcomers. We knock down obstacles and jump over hurdles. We endure fierce storms and fiery trials. We rise above the mountains that stand in our way. Because of the Holy Spirit, who lives inside of us, we triumph over anything the world brings our way. God's Spirit in us is greater than the evil that lives in the world. In Jesus we are more than conquerors and we have the victory. Praise the Lord!

Manna Moment

Think about your most recent trial and the wonderful way of escape God provided for you. Let your past victories be fibers of strength for present and future hardships.

Day 359: Know and Show

Dear friends, let us love one another, for love comes from God. Everyone who loves has been born of God and knows God.

And so we know and rely on the love God has for us. God is love. Whoever lives in love lives in God, and God in him.

—1 John 4:7, 16 (NIV)

The love the LORD has for us is the greatest love of all. Everyday should be a celebration of His love. His love is unconditional. That means that no mater what we do, He still loves us. His love is perfect and casts out all fear. There is no end to the love He has for us. And there is nothing that can separate us from His love.

The two greatest commandments are to love the LORD, with all of our heart, soul, mind and strength and to love our neighbors as we love ourselves. In 1 Corinthians, the Apostle Paul says that out of faith, hope and love, love is the greatest. May you know the love of the LORD and show His love to whoever God brings your way.

Manna Moment

Choose someone you know and show them the love of God.

Day 360: Ask Anything

This is the confidence we have in approaching God: that if we ask anything according to his will, he hears us. And if we know that he hears us—whatever we ask—we know that we have what we asked of him.
                    —1 John 5:14-15 (NIV)

We can know without a shadow of doubt, that when we ask God for anything in line with His will for us, His ear will be open to hear our request. Once He hears our request we can be certain we have received what we asked of Him. Notice it does not say we *will* have. The Word says we have it (notice the present tense). In God's perspective, it is already a done deal. We just have to stand in faith waiting for it to manifest.

Manna Moment

What do you need to ask God for today? Approach Him with confidence and believe you have received.

Day 361: Love = Obedience

And this is love: that we walk in obedience to his commands. As you have heard from the beginning, his command is that you walk in love.

—2 John 6 (NIV)

If we love the LORD we will walk in obedience to His commands. He has commanded us to walk in love. He is to be our first love and along with that, we are to love one another. The use of the word *walk* indicates that love is to be a continual, consistent action. Wherever we go we are to allow love to pour out of us. We are to love our neighbors, our enemies, our spouse, our children, other believers, unbelievers and ourselves.

The other side of the coin is to accept the love shown to us by others. When someone reaches out to us in love we want to accept their act of kindness and respond with thanksgiving. It is not meant to make us feel obligated. If we do not accept the kind acts of others, for whatever reason, we are not allowing the other person to be obedient. We are hindering their walk of obedience with the LORD. So walking in love involves the giving and receiving of love.

Manna Moment

Have you ever declined to accept an act of kindness that was shown to you? If so, think about why. Maybe, you did not feel you deserved it. Or maybe, you did not want to feel obligated to return the favor. Whatever the reason, make a decision to accept the kind deeds of others so you both can be blessed.

Day 362: Prosperity and Health

Beloved, I pray that in all respects you may prosper and be in good health, just as your soul prospers.
—3 John 2 (NAS)

Prosperity refers to a very positive state of affairs. It is not limited to wealth, but also encompasses success and favor. Just as John, the apostle of Jesus Christ, prayed for his friend and fellow believer, Gaius, I offer a blessing and prayer to my beloved readers and fellow believers.

I pray you would be in good health, full of strength and vigor. In addition, I pray your soul would be at peace and overflow with joy. May the LORD bless all you put your hand to with success. I pray that the rest of your life would be the best of your life. Amen.

Manna Moment

How would you like to have prosperity manifest in your life? Write down what you would like to do, what you want to be and what you want to have. Present your desires to the LORD and believe that in His due time you will receive.

Day 363: He is Able to Keep You

To him who is able to keep you from falling and to present you before his glorious presence without fault and with great joy - to the only God our Savior be glory, majesty, power and authority, through Jesus Christ our Lord, before all ages, now and forevermore! Amen.

—Jude 24-25 (NIV)

When you become weak and weary, our God is able to keep you from falling. If you get tripped up while running your race, He is able to keep you from falling. You can rely on our glorious, majestic and powerful God to give the strength and balance you need to remain standing in Him. And you will be without fault and bursting with joy as you stand in His presence.

Manna Moment

In times of gloom and doom lay your concerns in the lap of the LORD and appreciate the fact that He is able to keep you from falling.

Day 364: Here I Am!

"Those whom I love I rebuke and discipline. So be earnest, and repent. Here I am! I stand at the door and knock. If anyone hears my voice and opens the door, I will come in and eat with him, and he with me."
—Revelation 3:19-20 (NIV)

First, we need to repent of anything that is not of God in our lives. We should turn our backs to it and face toward Jesus. Secondly, we have to listen for His voice. Sometimes it is a soft, gentle whisper and sometimes it comes through as clear and loud as thunder. Third, we are to open the door of our hearts to Him and keep it open. As we give more and more of our hearts to Jesus we become increasingly more like Him. We experience wonderful fellowship with our Lord and Savior, Jesus Christ.

May you hear His voice today and open the door to your heart. Enjoy a wonderful feast with Him today. He is here!

Manna Moment

Walk through your house today and prepare it for Jesus to come in and dine with you. When you are finished, open your door and invite Him in. Talk to Him as you would your closest friend.

Day 365: In a War

When the dragon saw that he had been hurled to the earth, he pursued the woman who had given birth to the male child....

Then the dragon was enraged at the woman and went off to make war against the rest of her offspring—those who obey God's commandments and hold to the testimony of Jesus.

—Revelation 12:13, 17 (NIV)

This account in Revelations serves as a reminder that Christians are indeed in a war. Since we are the offspring of the woman, we are natural enemies to Satan. He wages war with every person who follows after God. Fear not, we are victorious in Jesus Christ. As the apostle Paul reminds us in Ephesians 6:12, our struggle is against the rulers, the authorities, the powers of this dark world and against spiritual forces of evil in the heavenly realms. Remember, our battles are not against flesh and blood. We are not fighting our spouses, children, parents, extended family members, in-laws, co-workers, bosses or neighbors. We are contending with the devil and his demons, so we have to fight our battles in the spirit, not in the flesh.

God equips us with a full armor and the precise weapon we need to fight, His Word. God's Word is the sword of the Spirit and it is alive and active. Use it! Send the devil fleeing by getting the Word in your spirit and speaking it out of your mouth. And pray at all times and in every situation. Though it may seem like the enemy has won a battle, our heavenly Father works everything together for good for those who love Him. Amen.

Manna Moment

Do you engage into battle with people? Do combat in the spiritual domain by speaking the Word over any conflicts that come your way. Praise God for the victory that is ours in Jesus Christ.

Day 366: The New Jerusalem

And I heard a loud voice from the throne saying, "Now the dwelling of God is with men, and he will live with them. They will be his people, and God himself will be with them and be their God. He will wipe every tear from their eyes. There will be no more death or mourning or crying or pain, for the old order of things has passed away."
—Revelation 21:3-4 (NIV)

God will take His hand and wipe all our tears away. There will be no more crying or pain or mourning. Death will have no power over us. We will not need the light of a lamp nor the light of the sun because the Lord God will give us light (Revelation 22:5). What a glorious future we have and it will be for all eternity. Endure the temporary trials of today with your mind set on the magnificent prize at the finish line.

Manna Moment

When things get difficult, think about the glorious future we have awaiting us. Visualize Jesus sitting on His throne in all His glory adorned with His radiant crown. Imagine the sound of multitudes of angels singing His praise. Picture yourself worshiping Jesus, the Lamb of God, the King of kings and the Lord of lords. See you there!

To receive the Manna in the Morning e-mails:

E-mail jackieharts@yahoo.com with "Send Me the Manna" in the subject line.

Printed in the United States
200661BV00001B/79-1023/A

9 781604 772159